See You S

またあうひまで

Bemojake

See You Soon

またあうひまで

October
2010

Maxwell Anderson

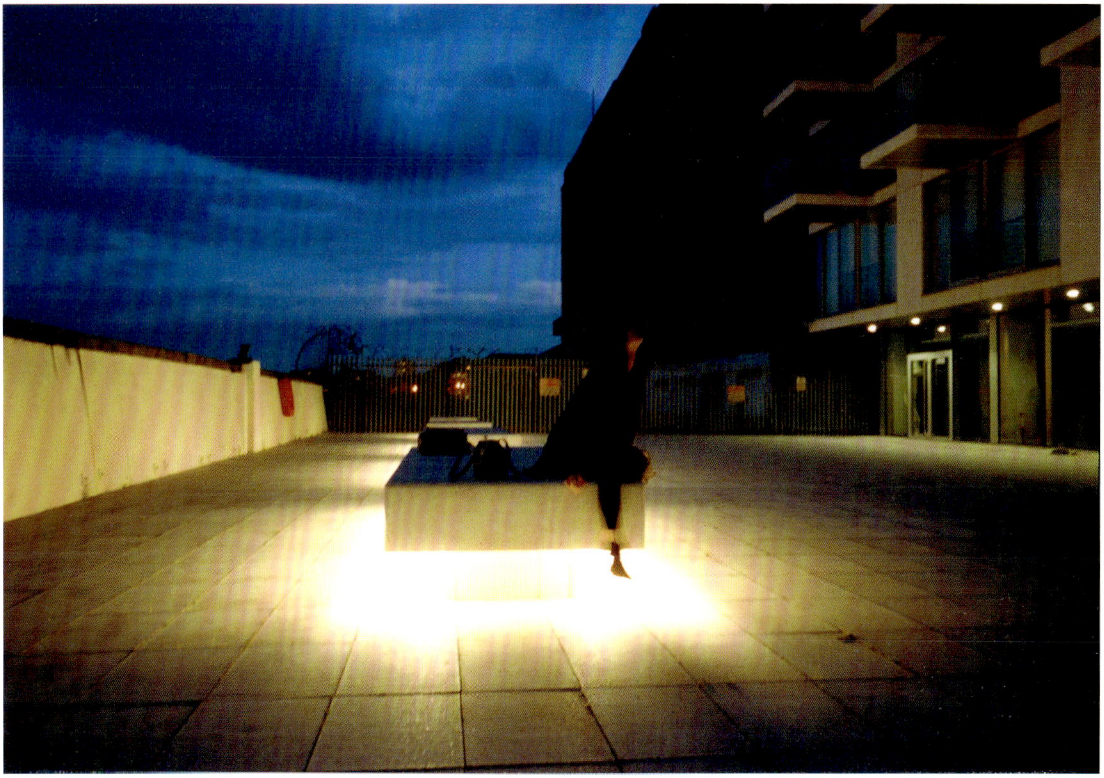

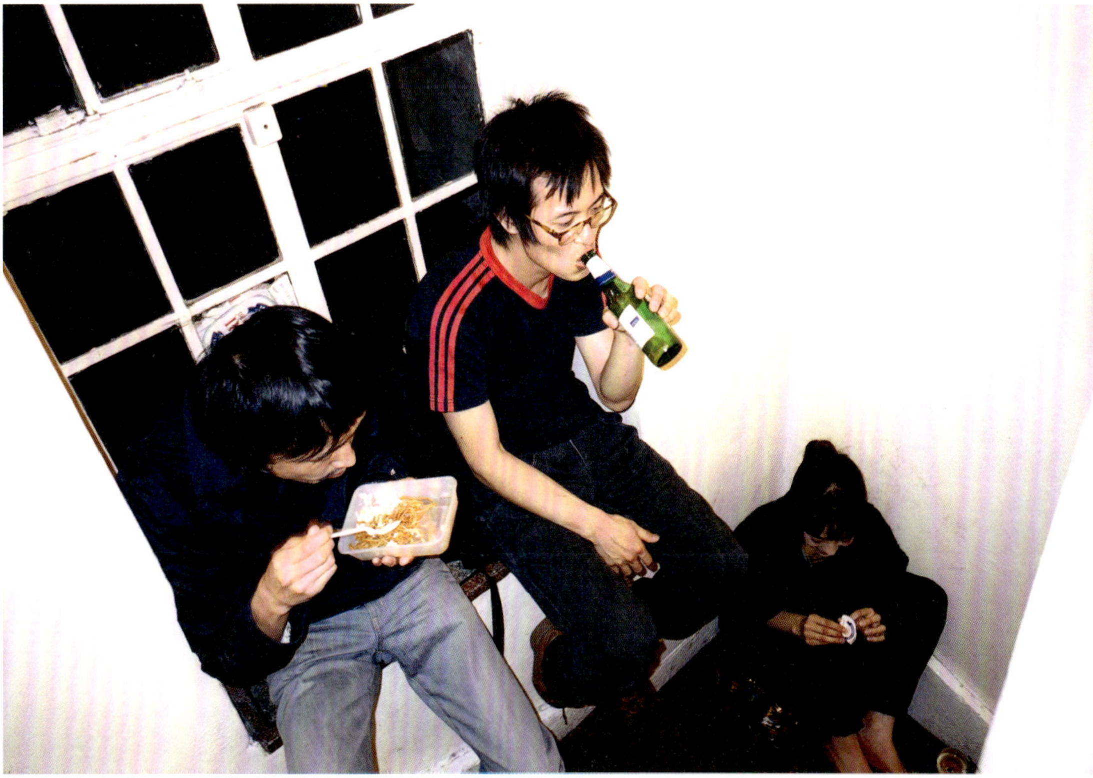

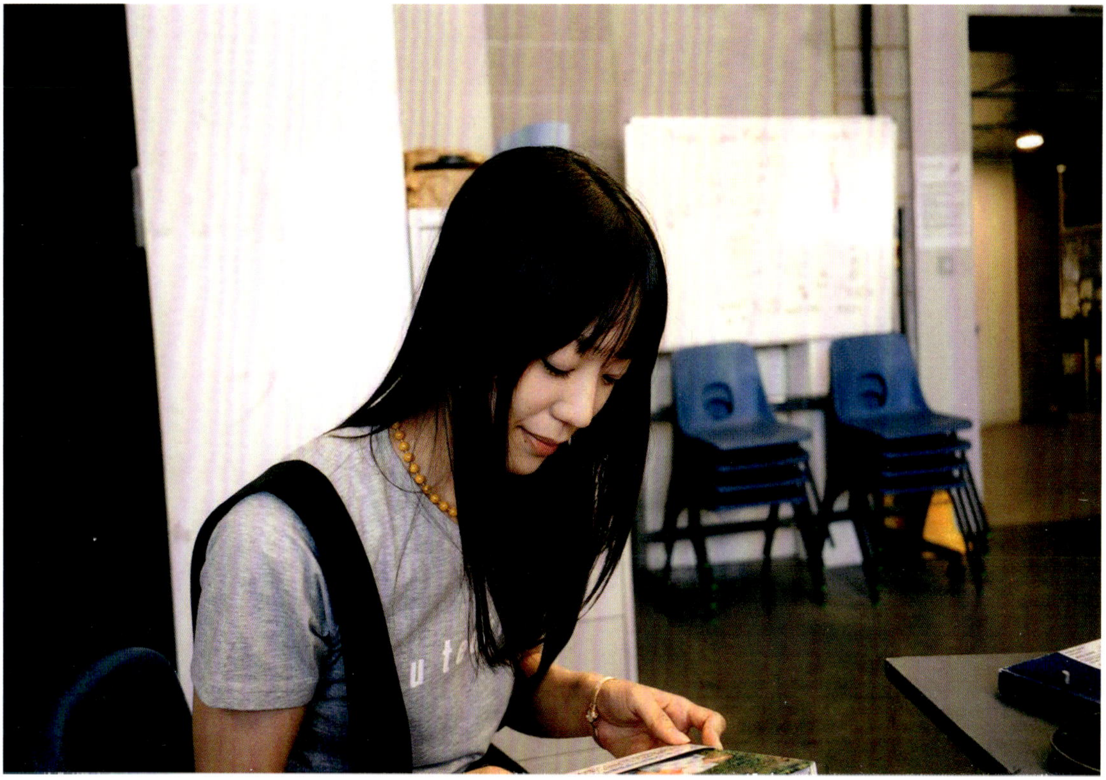

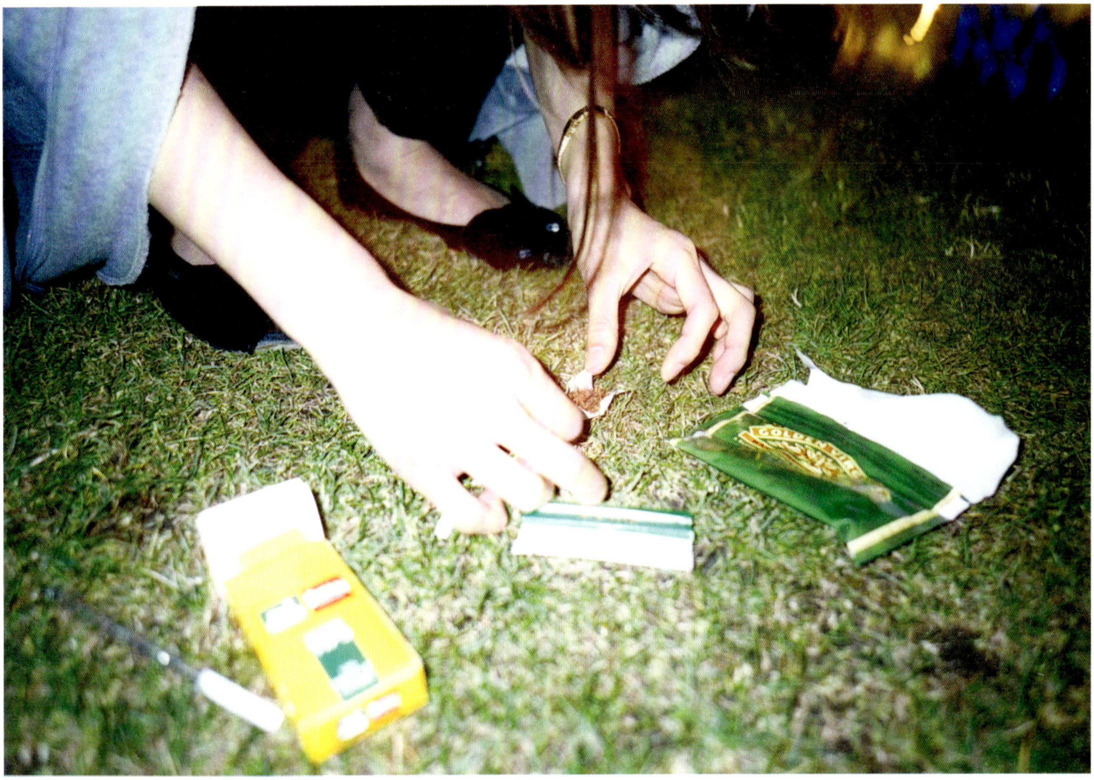

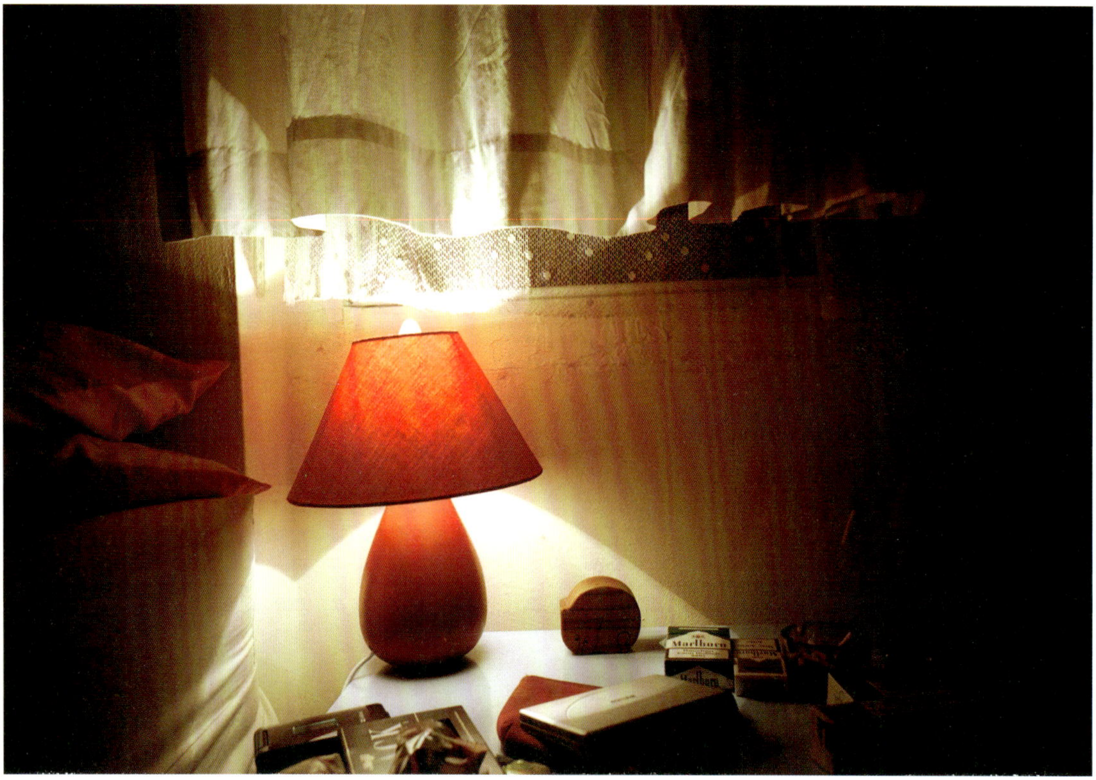
Marlboro

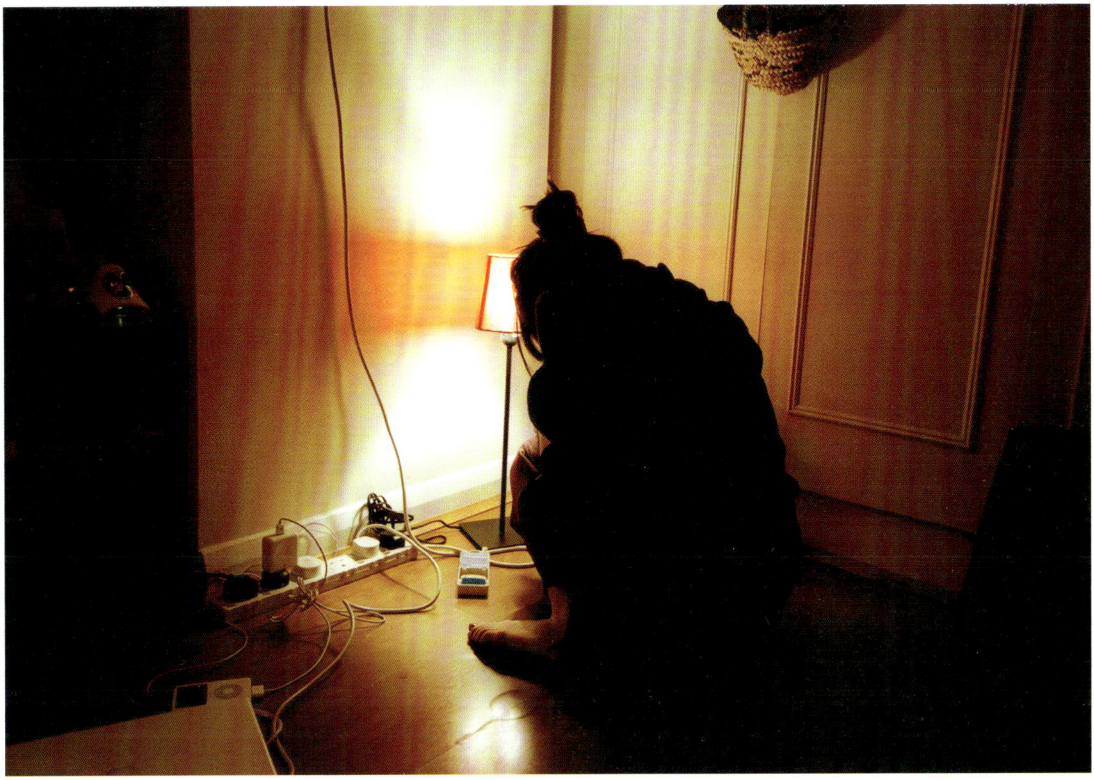

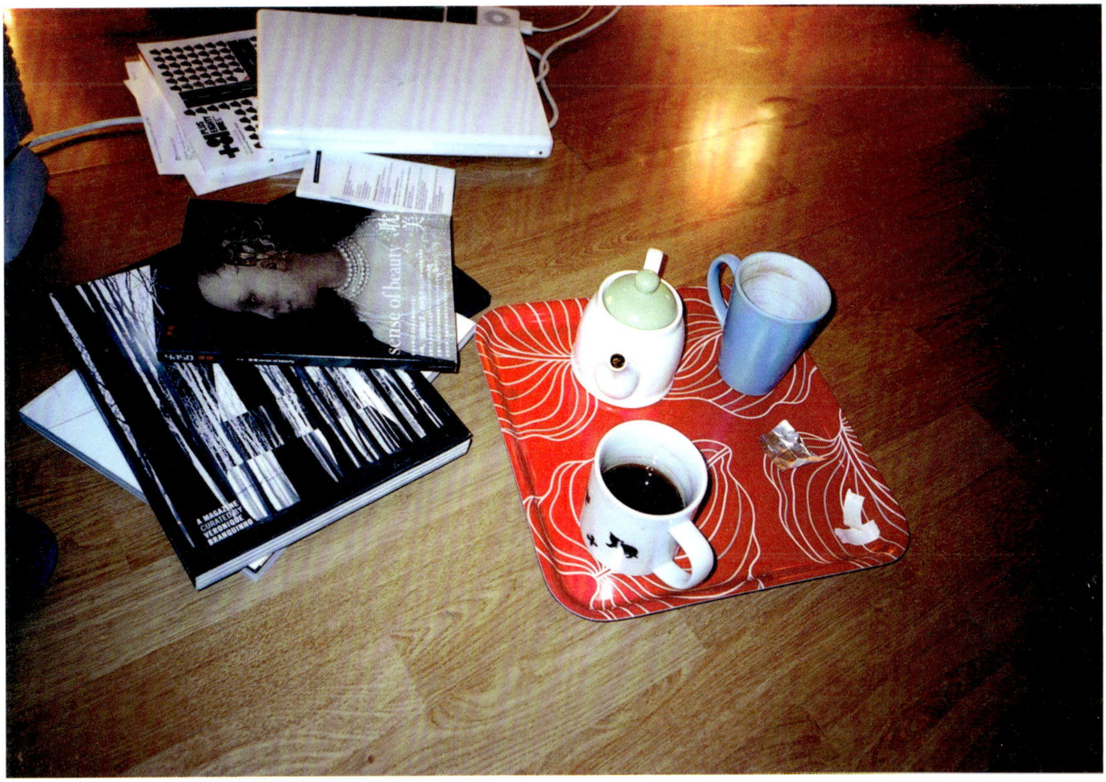
+81 PLUS EIGHTY ONE
sense of beauty
A MAGAZINE CURATED BY VERONIQUE BRANQUINHO

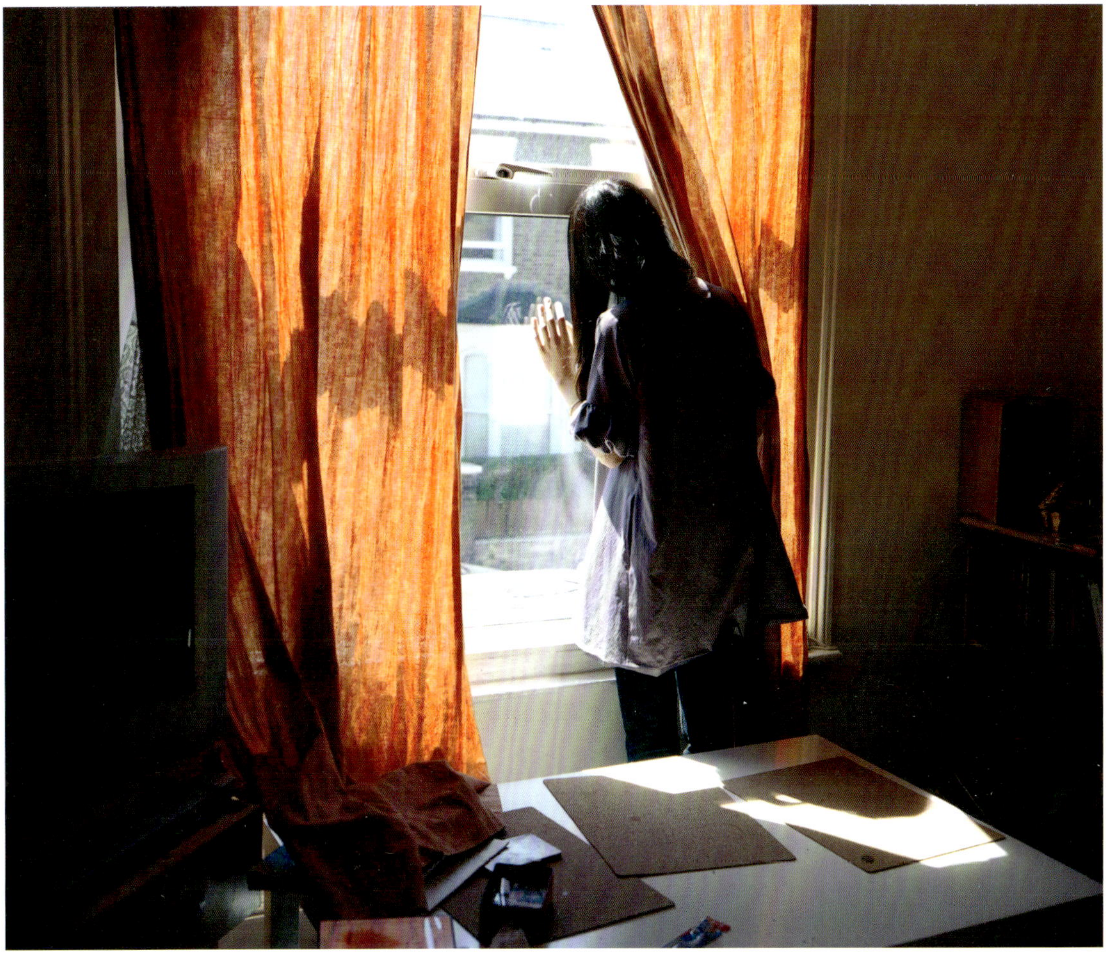

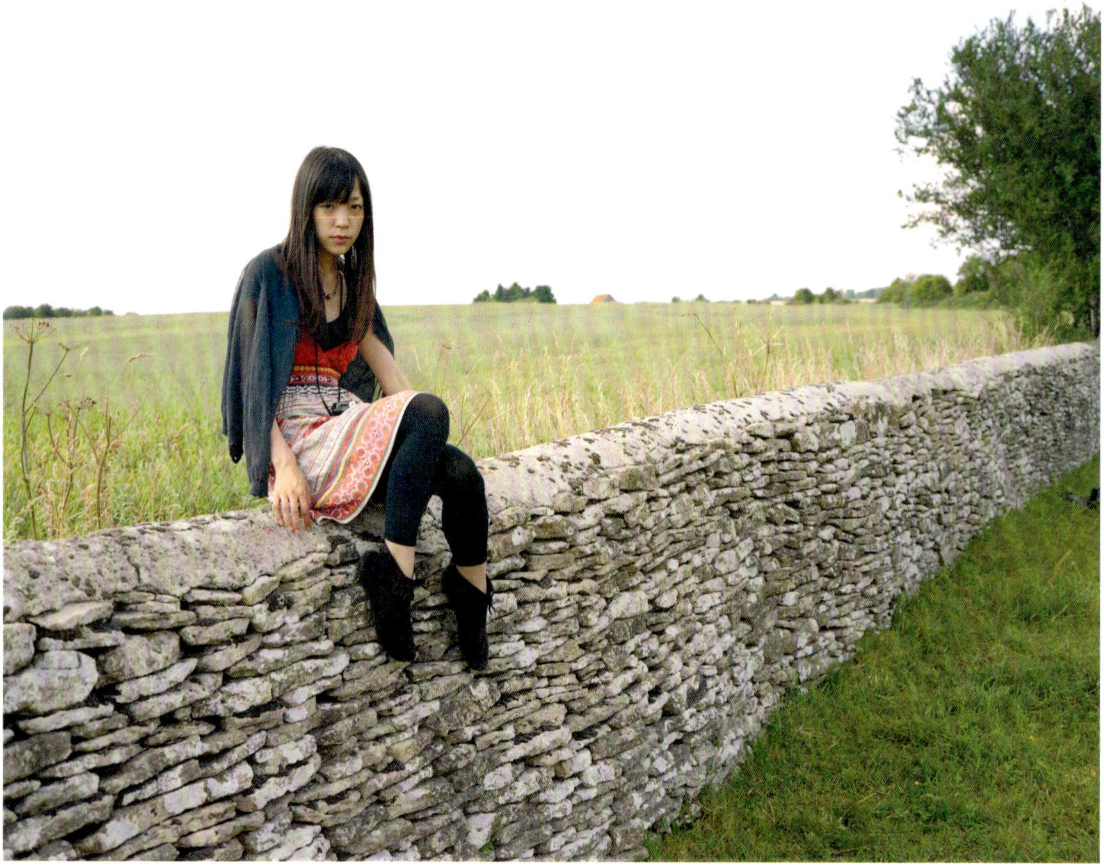

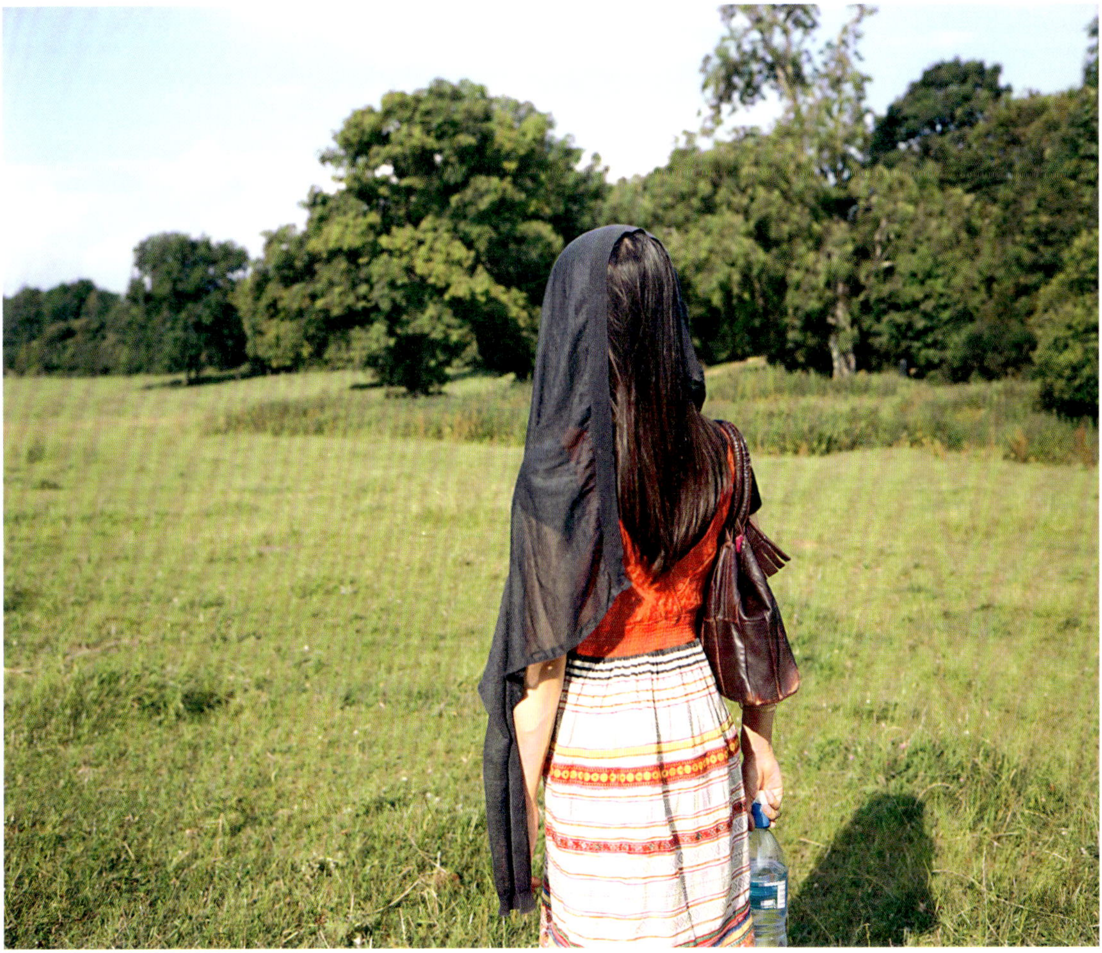

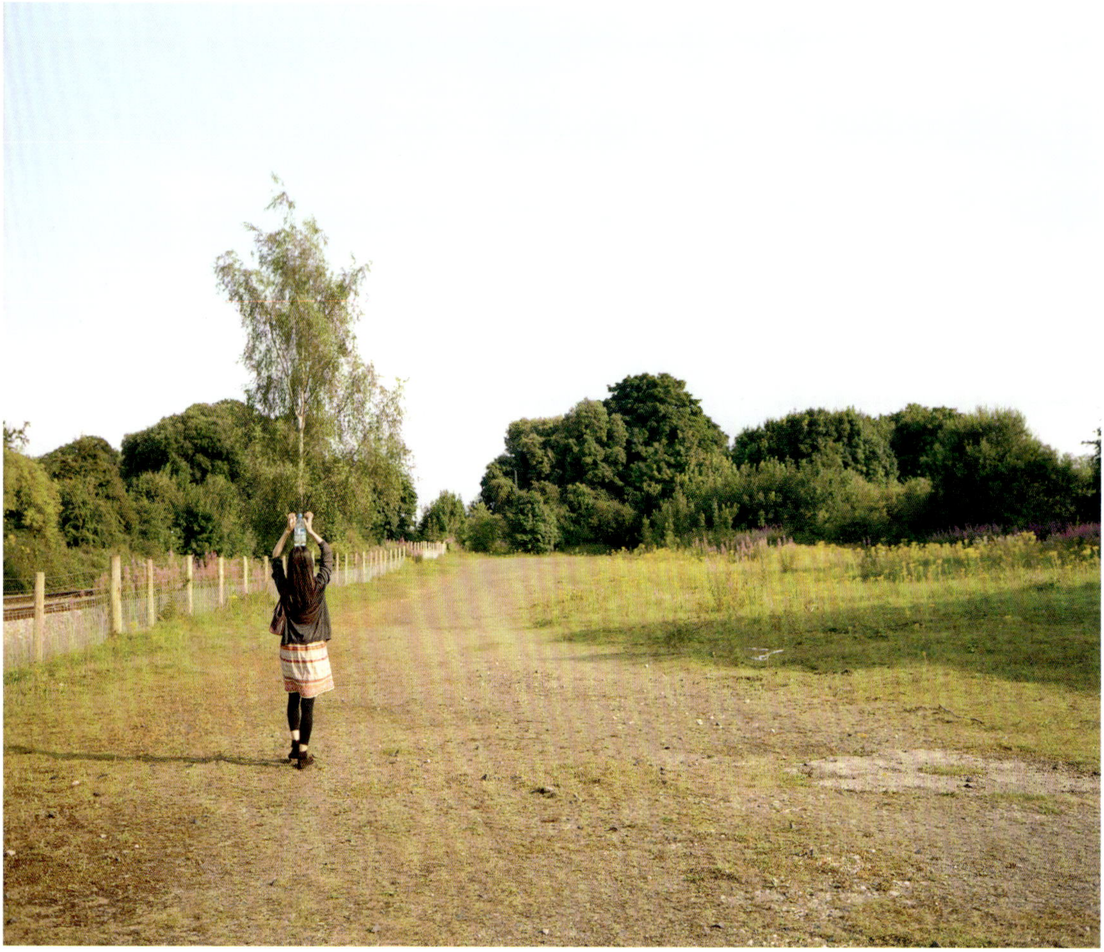

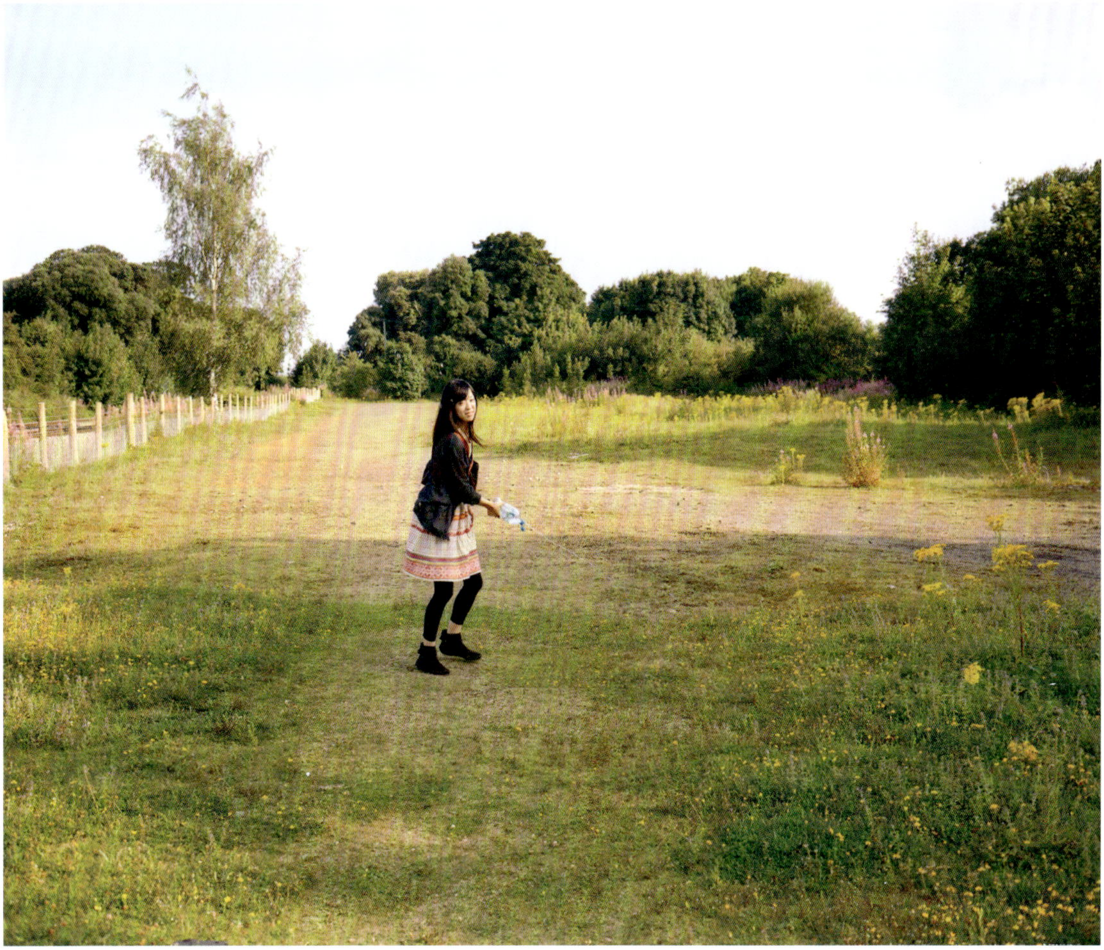

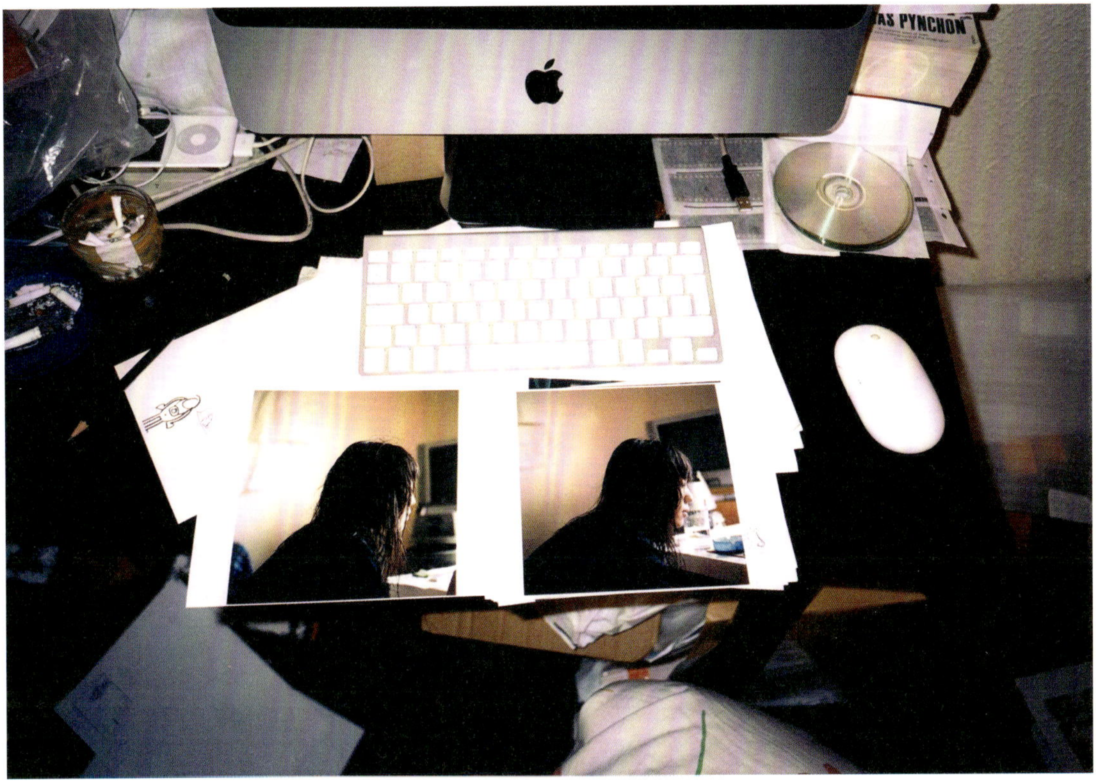
AS PYNCHON

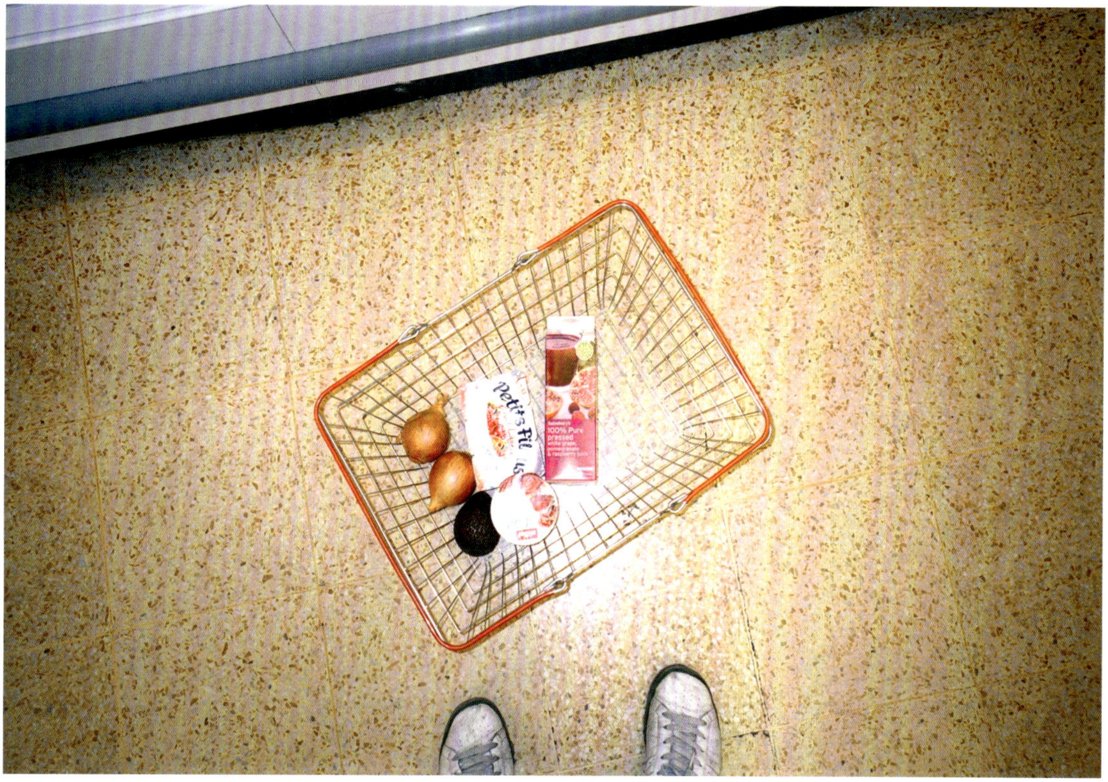
100% Pure
pressed

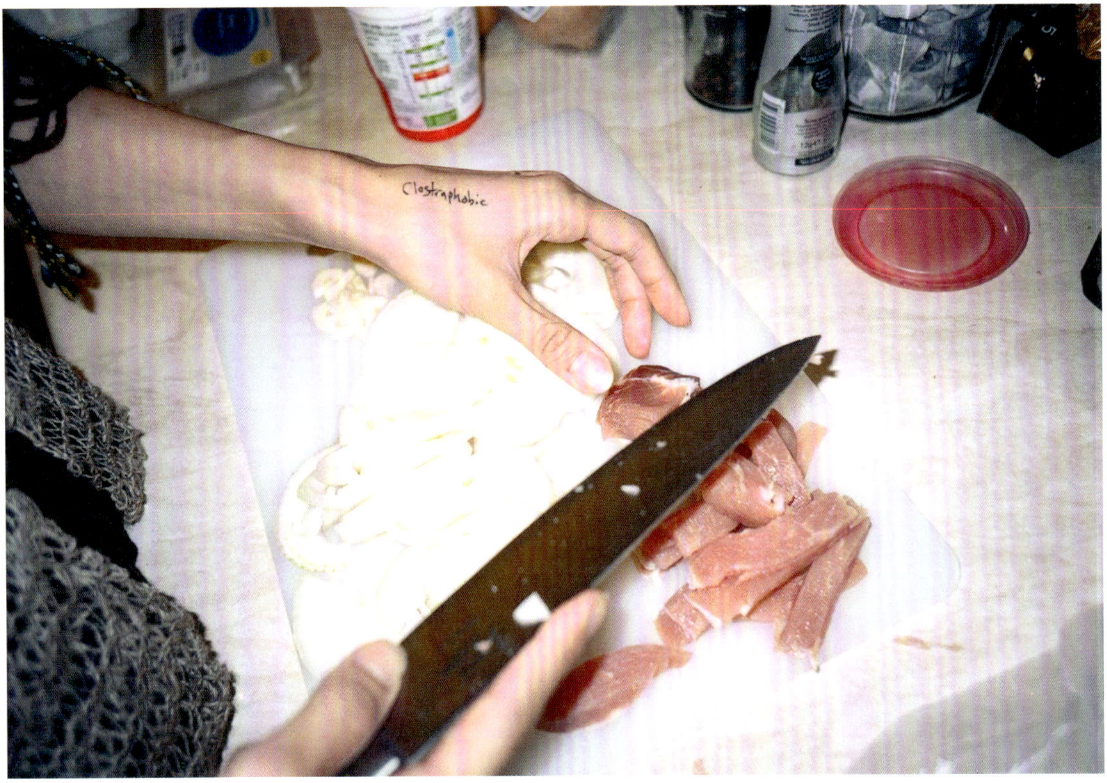
Clostraphobic

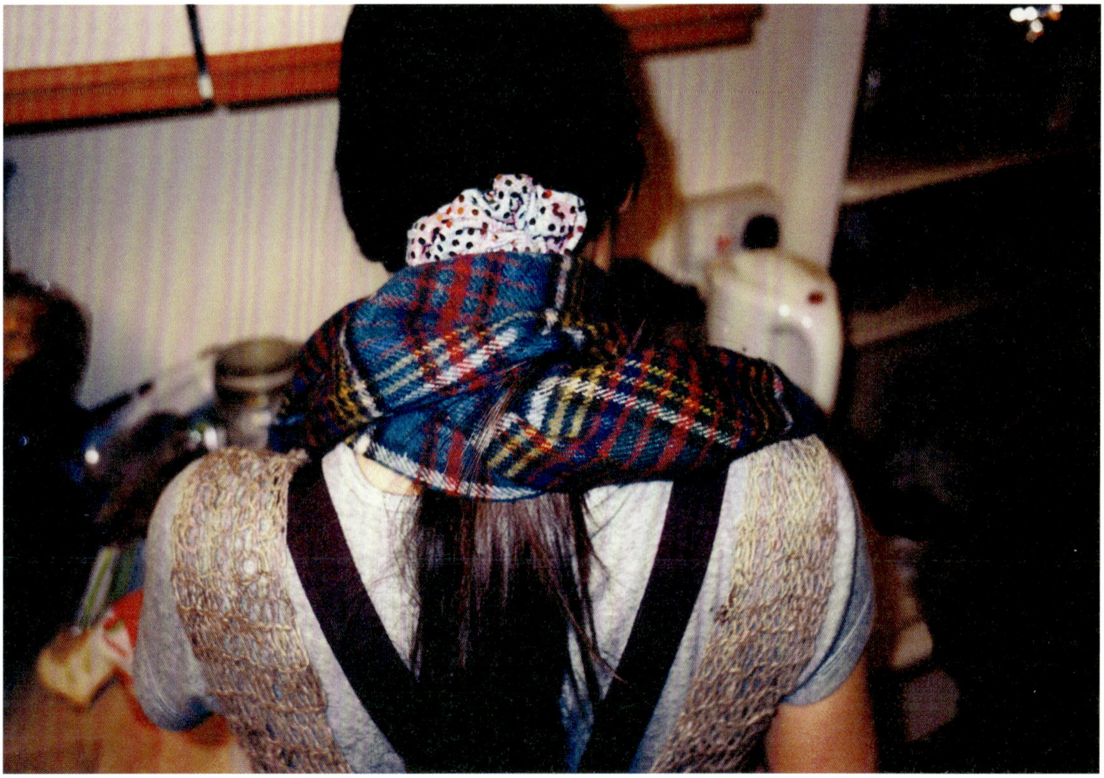

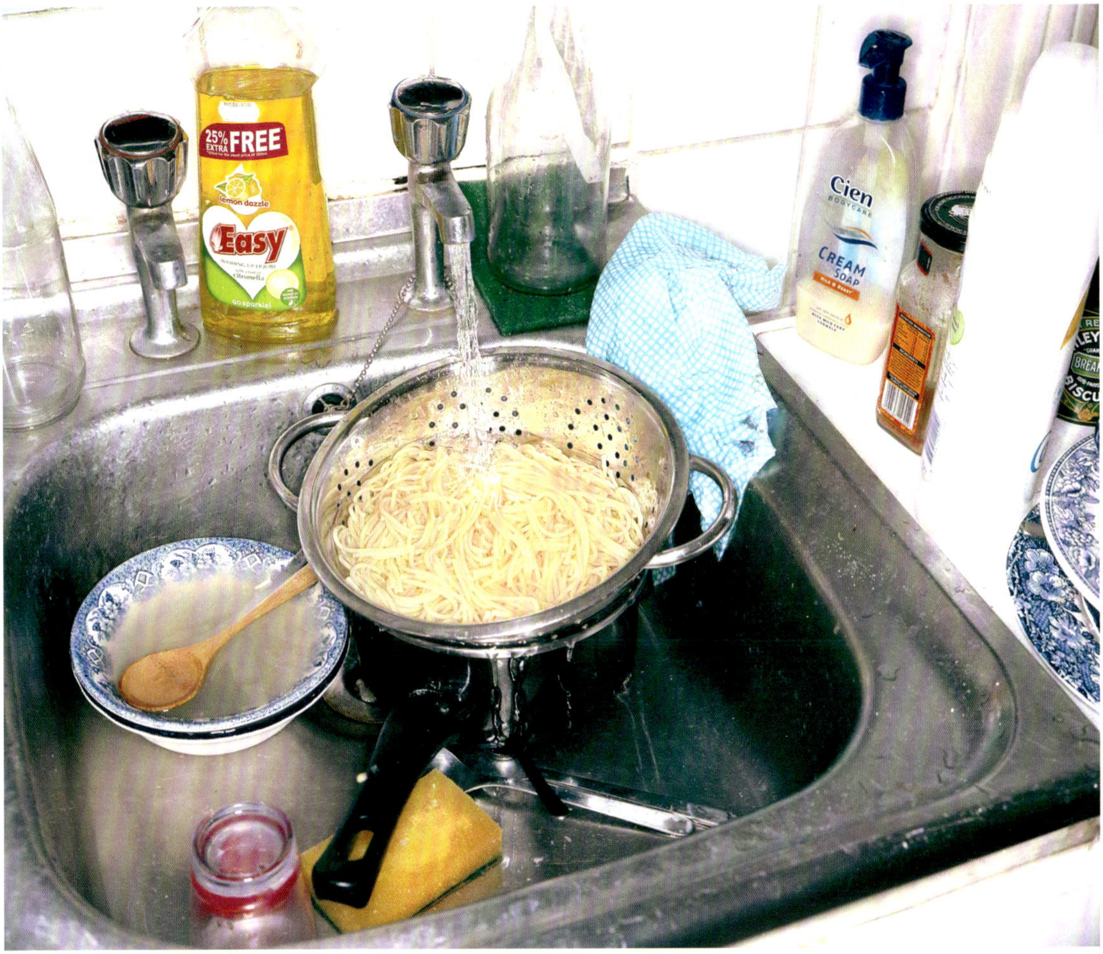
25% EXTRA FREE
lemon dazzle
Easy
Cien
BODYCARE
CREAM SOAP

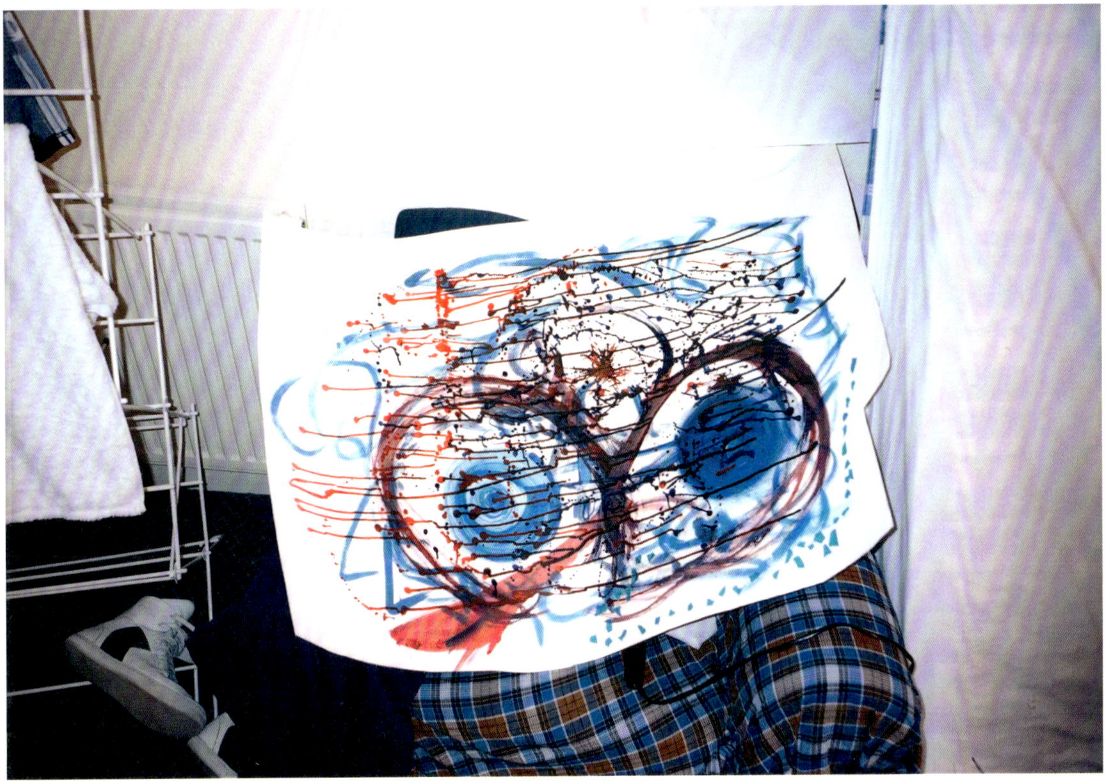

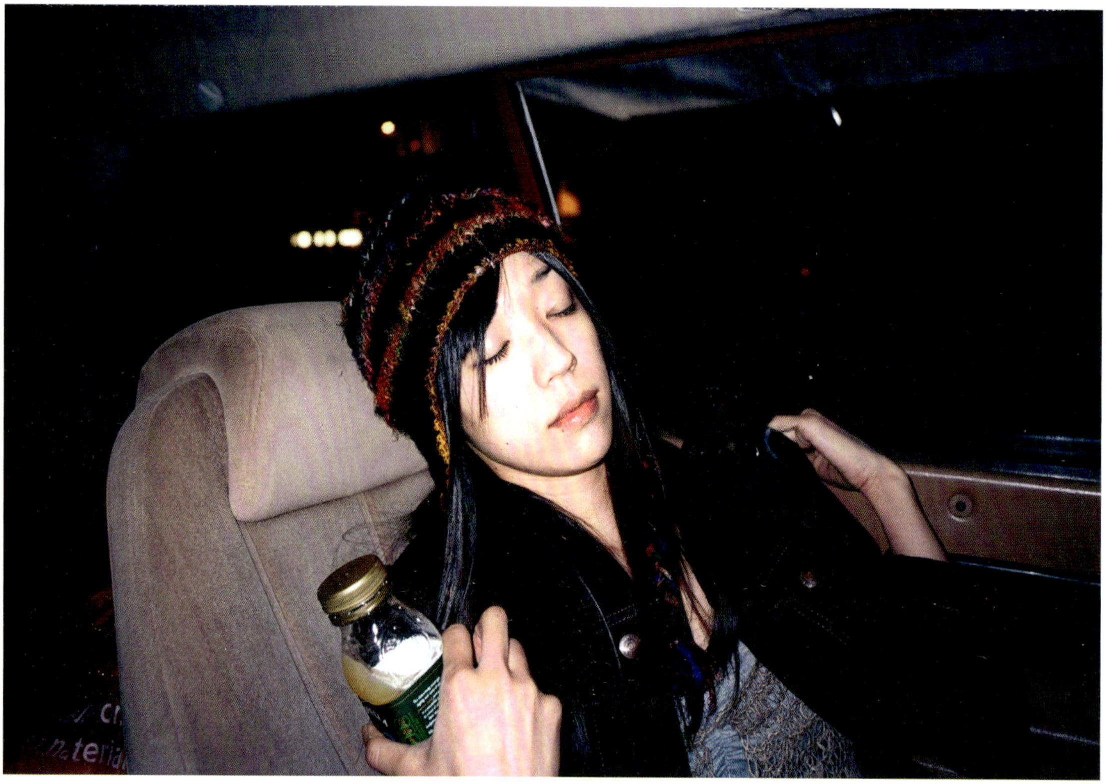

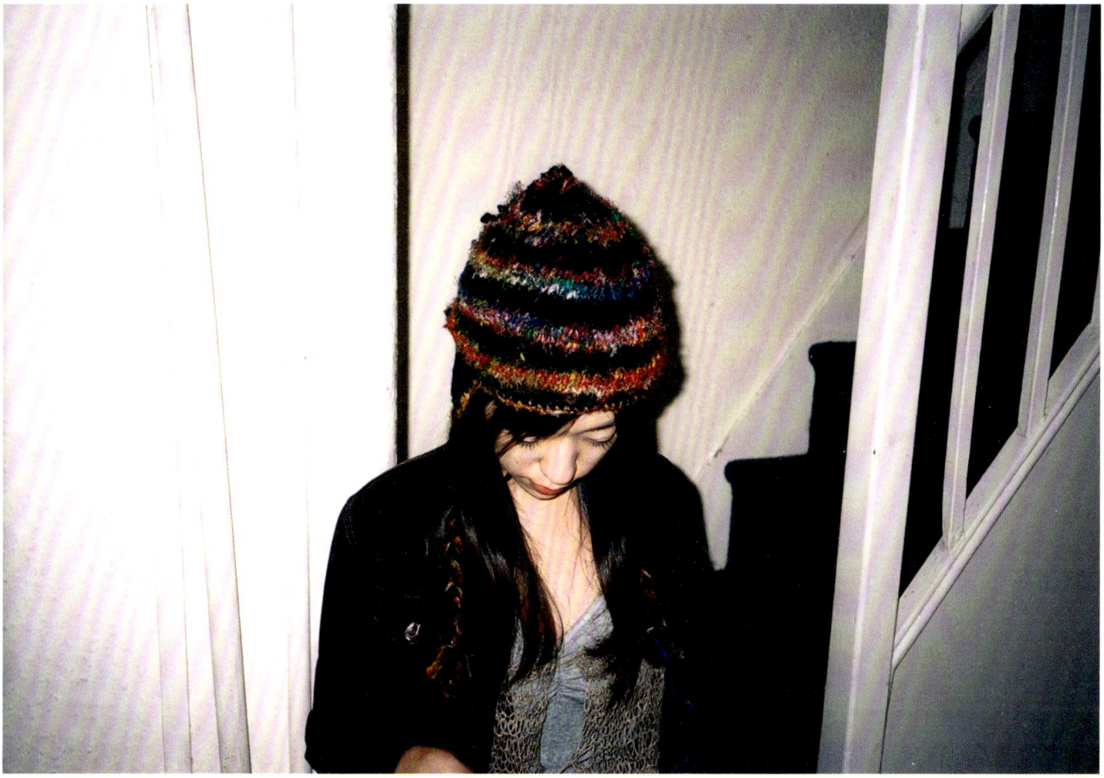

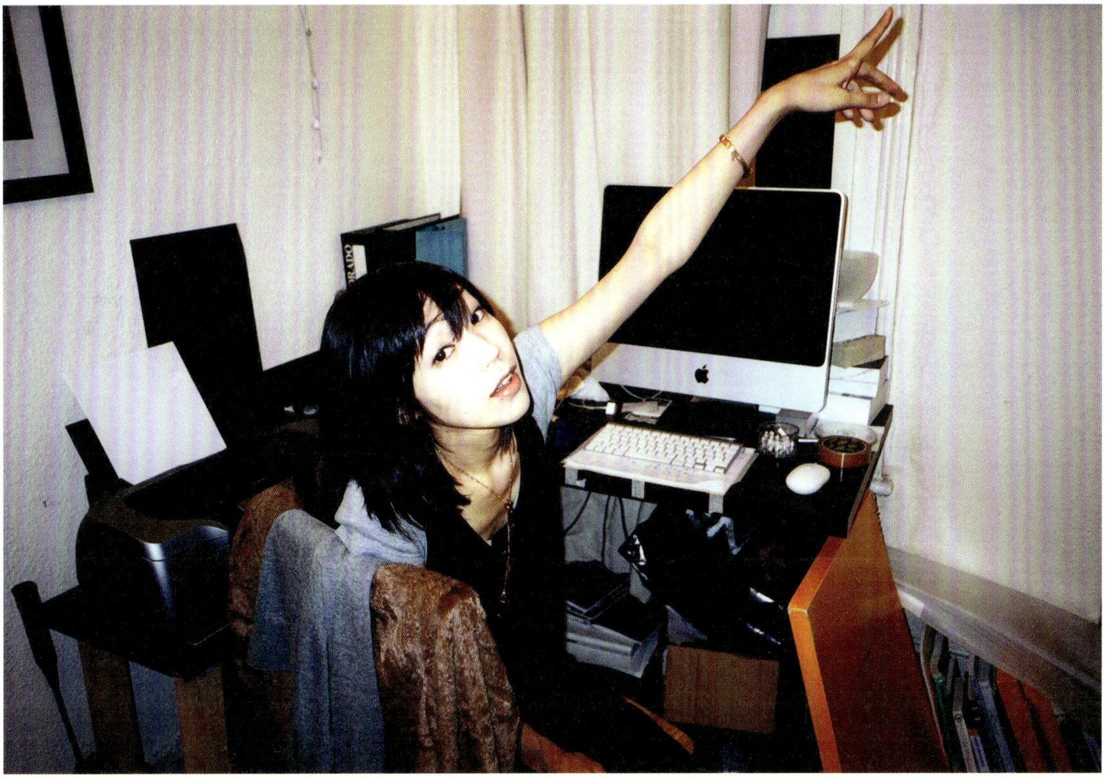

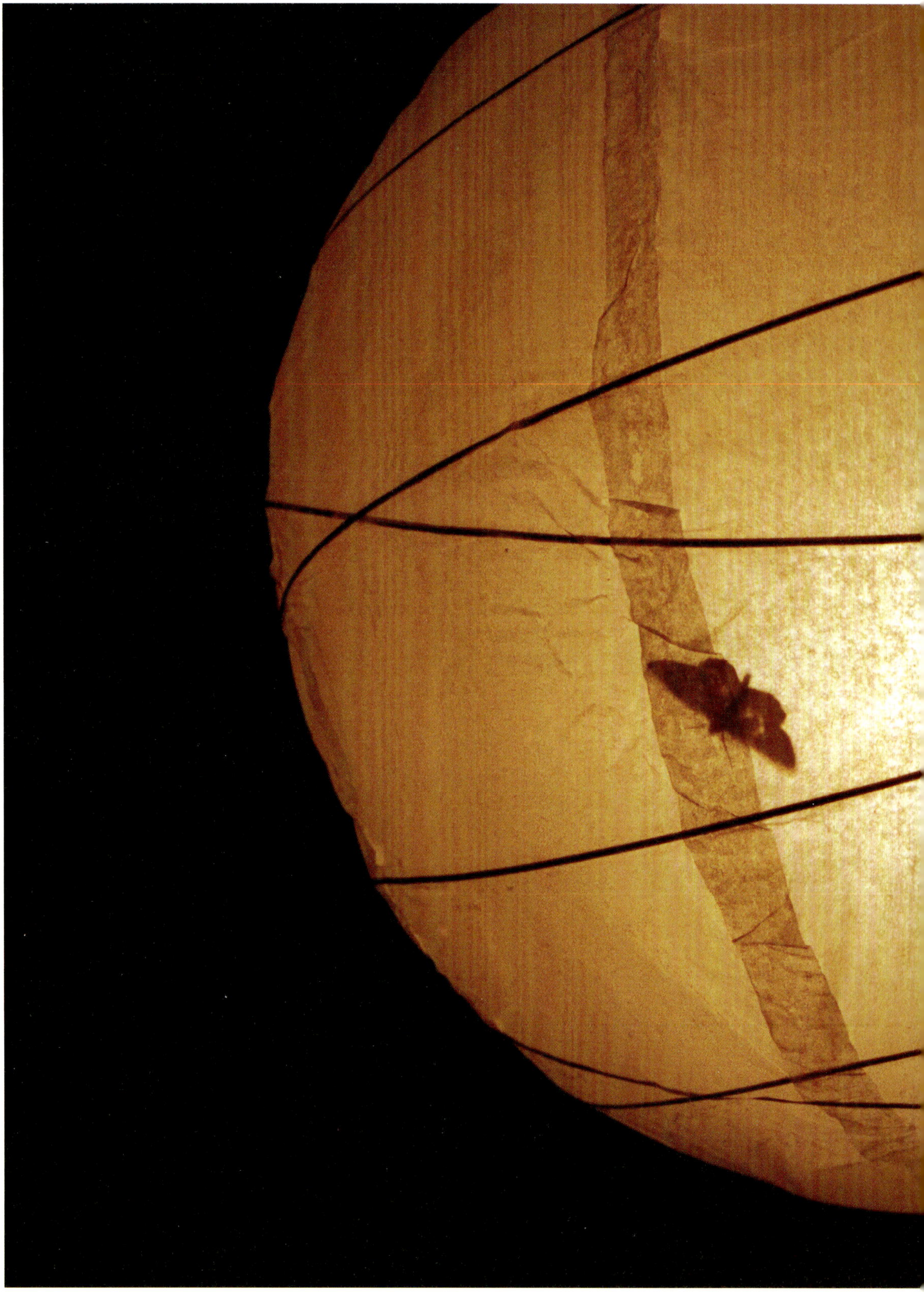

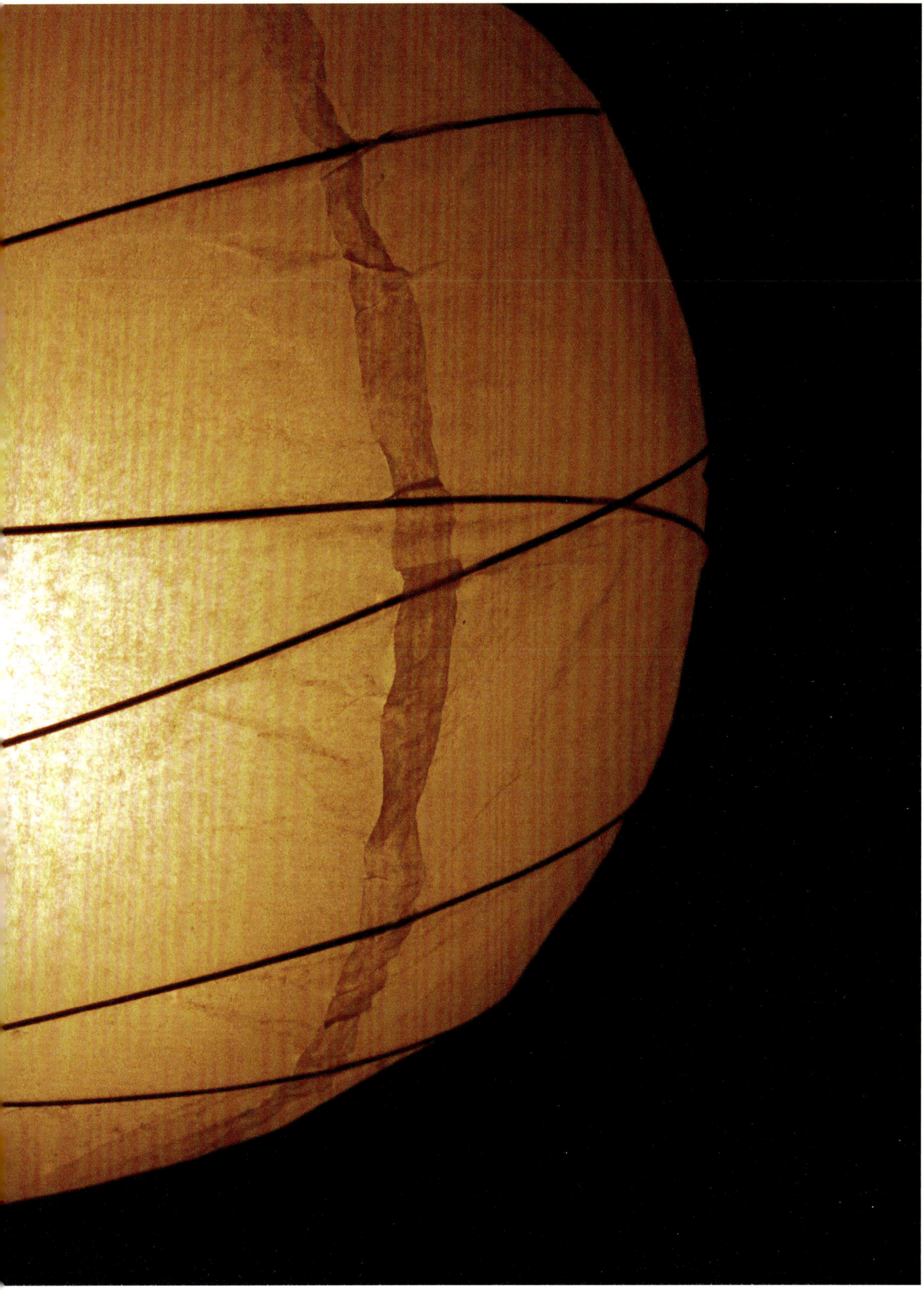

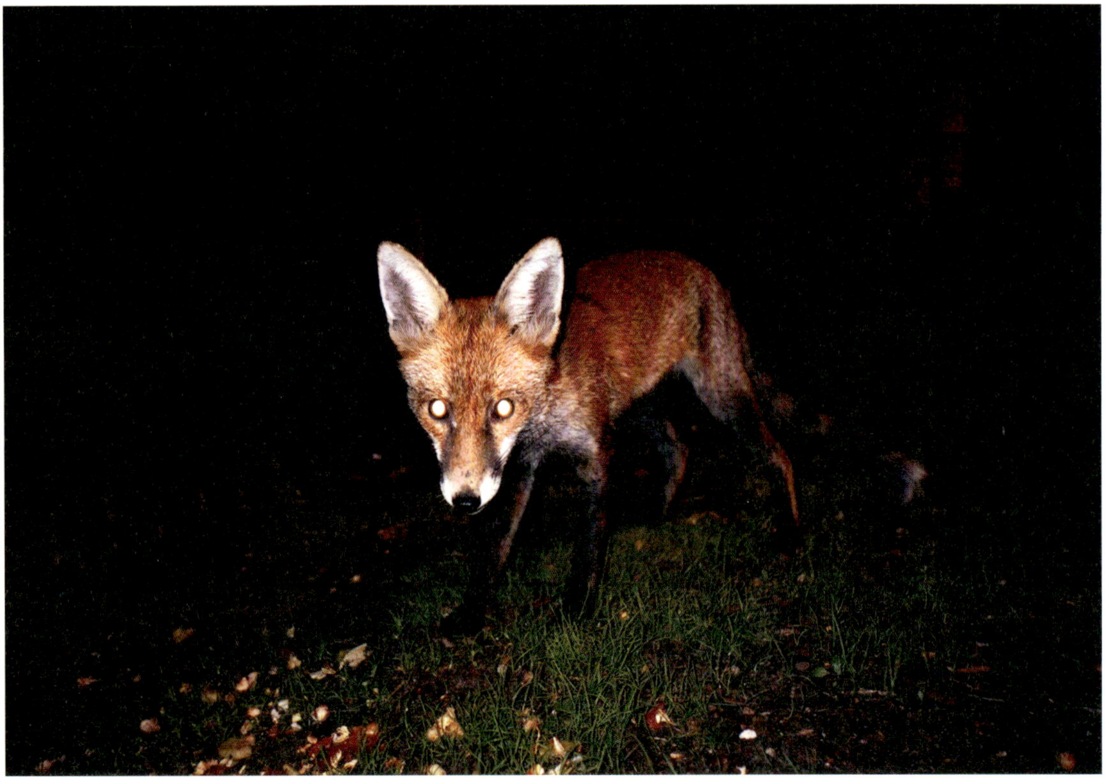

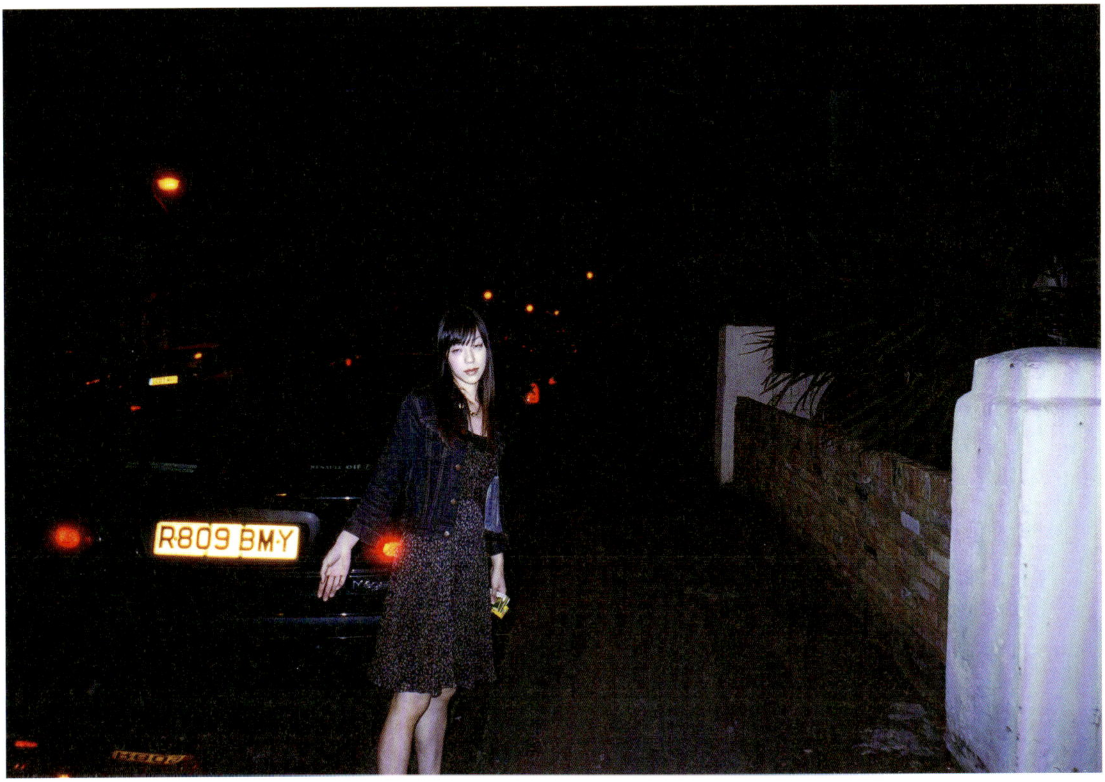
R809 BMY

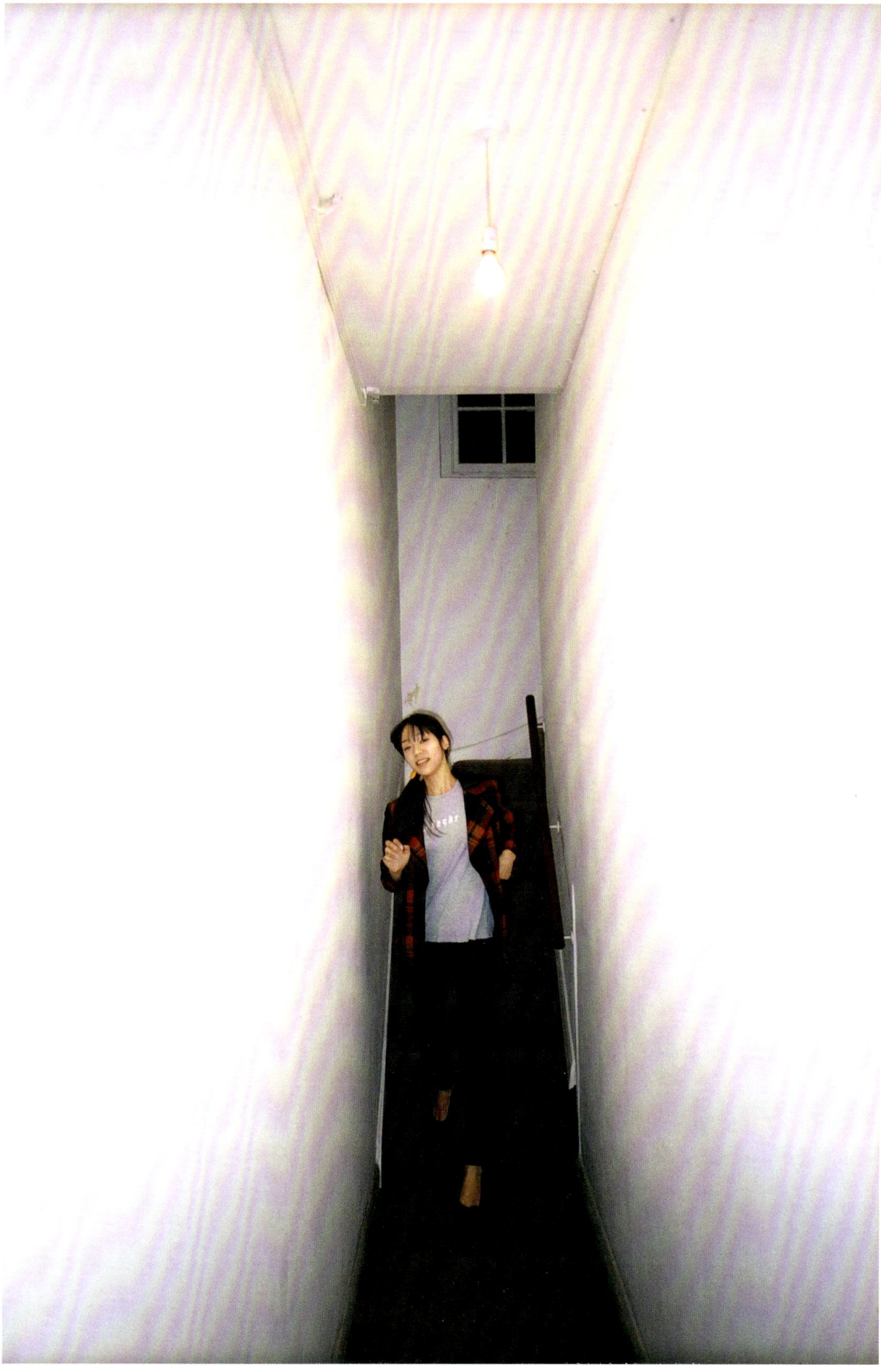

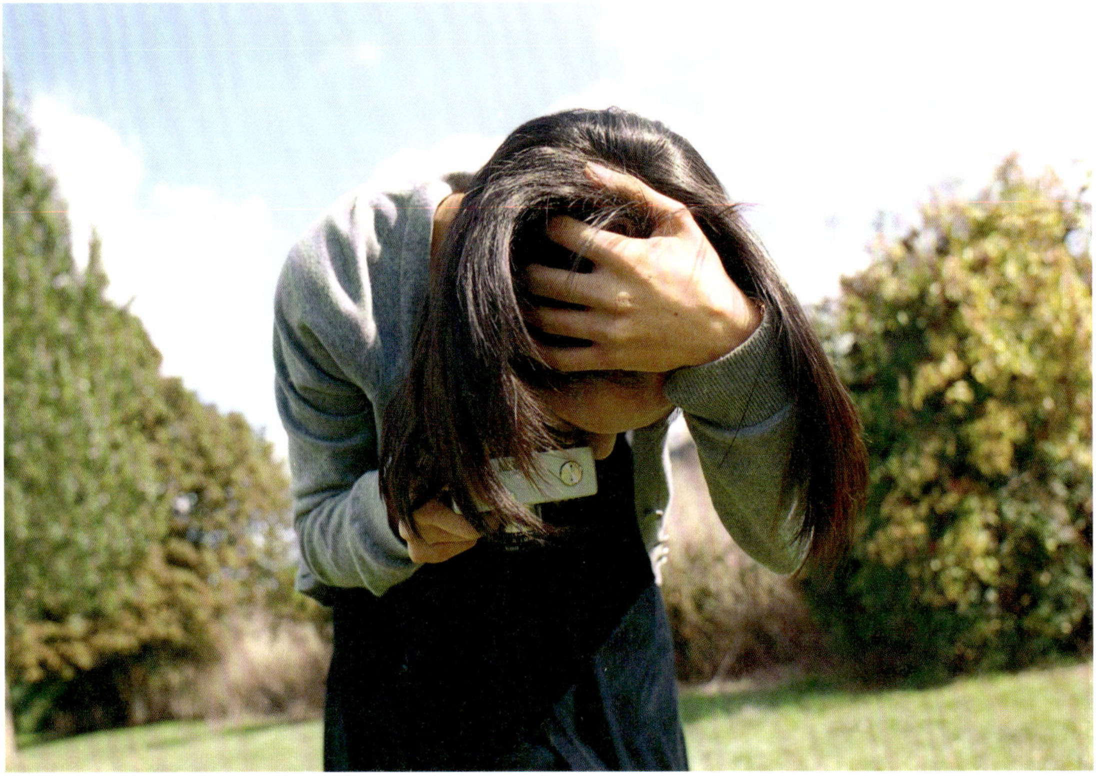

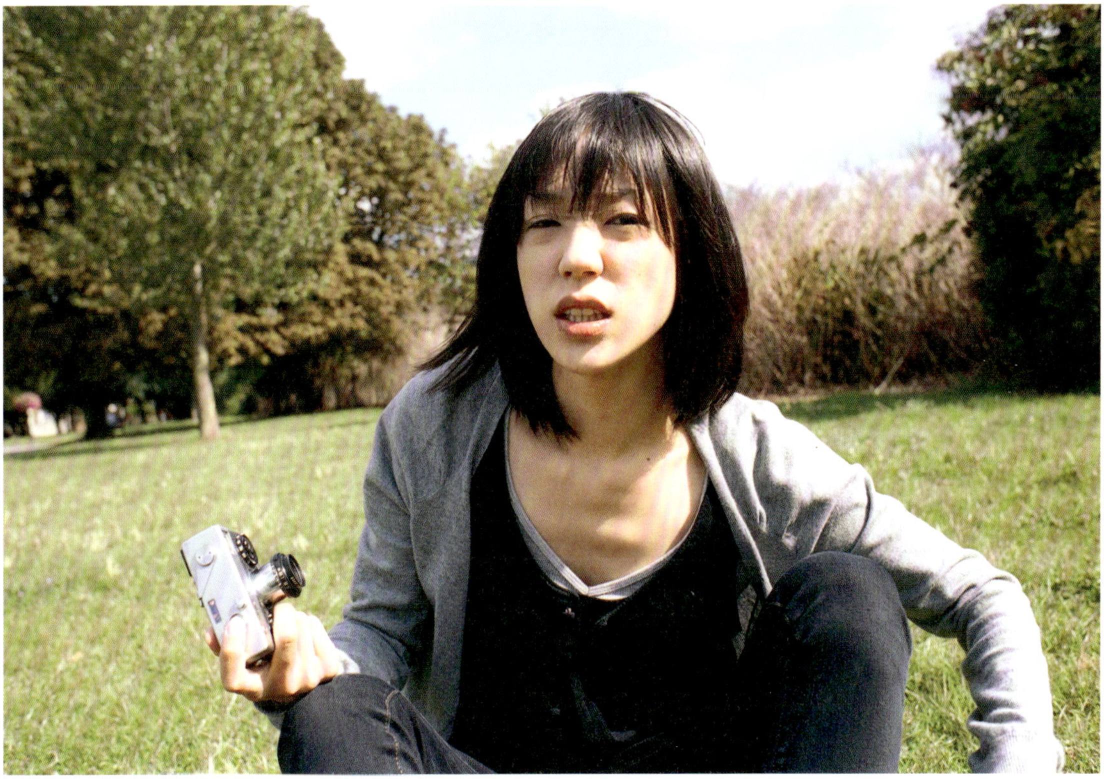

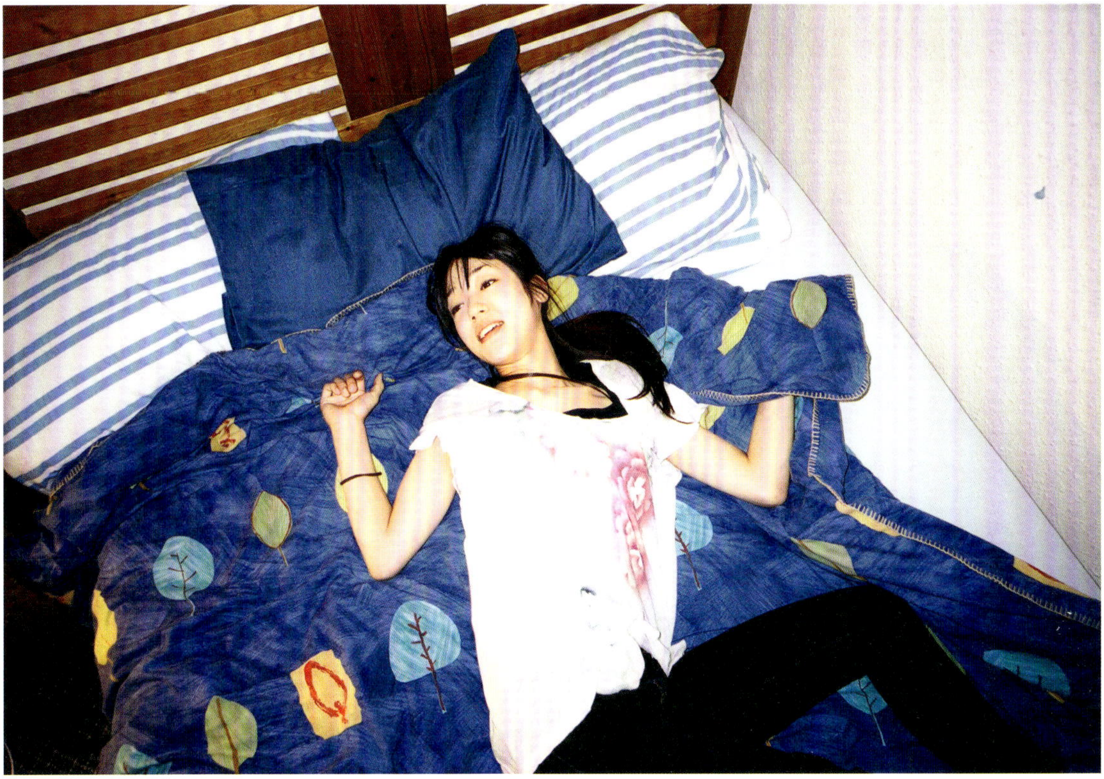

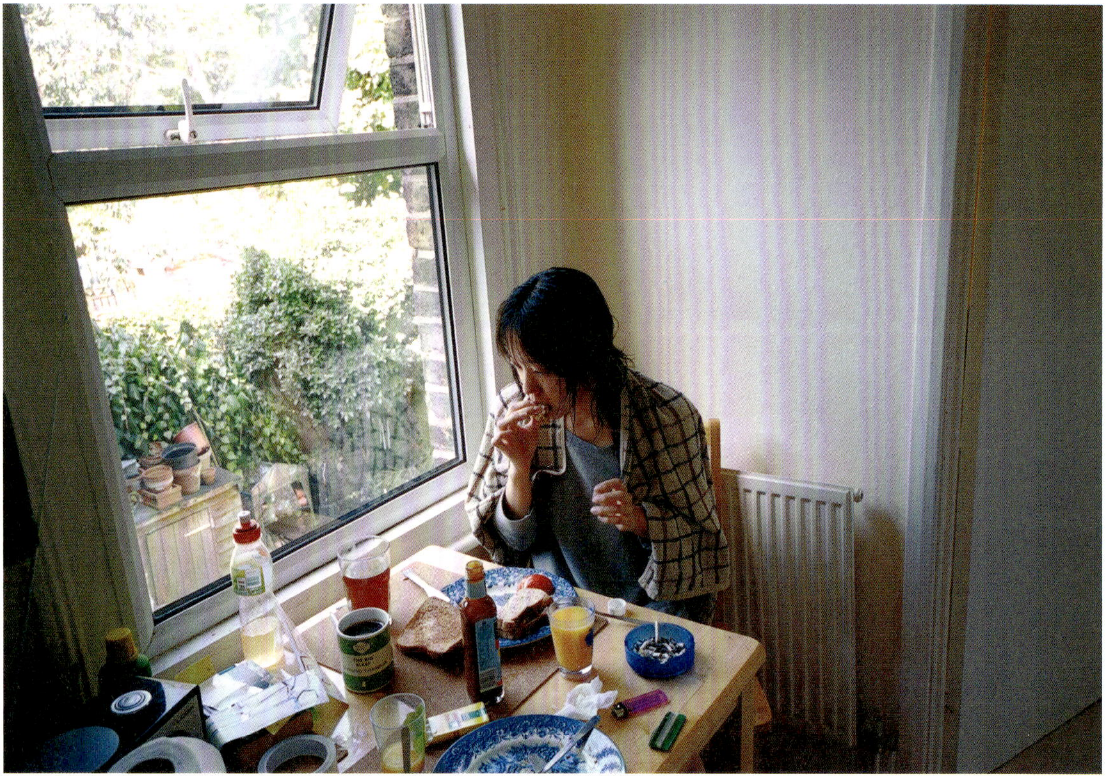

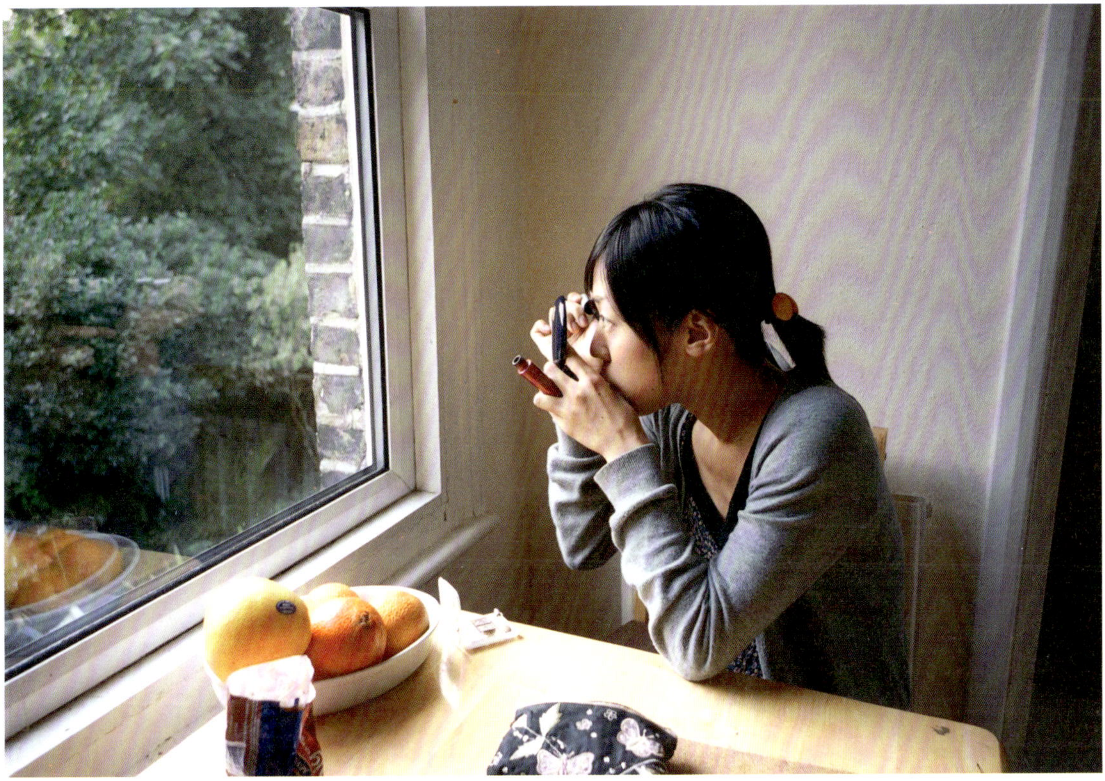

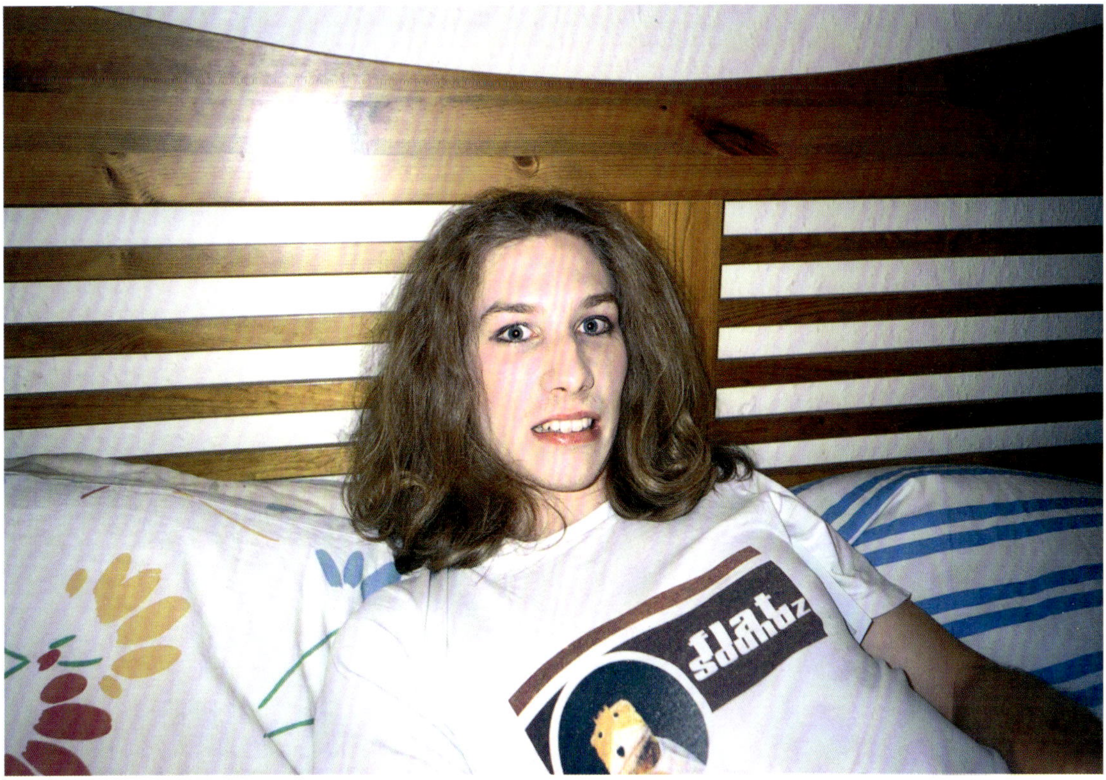

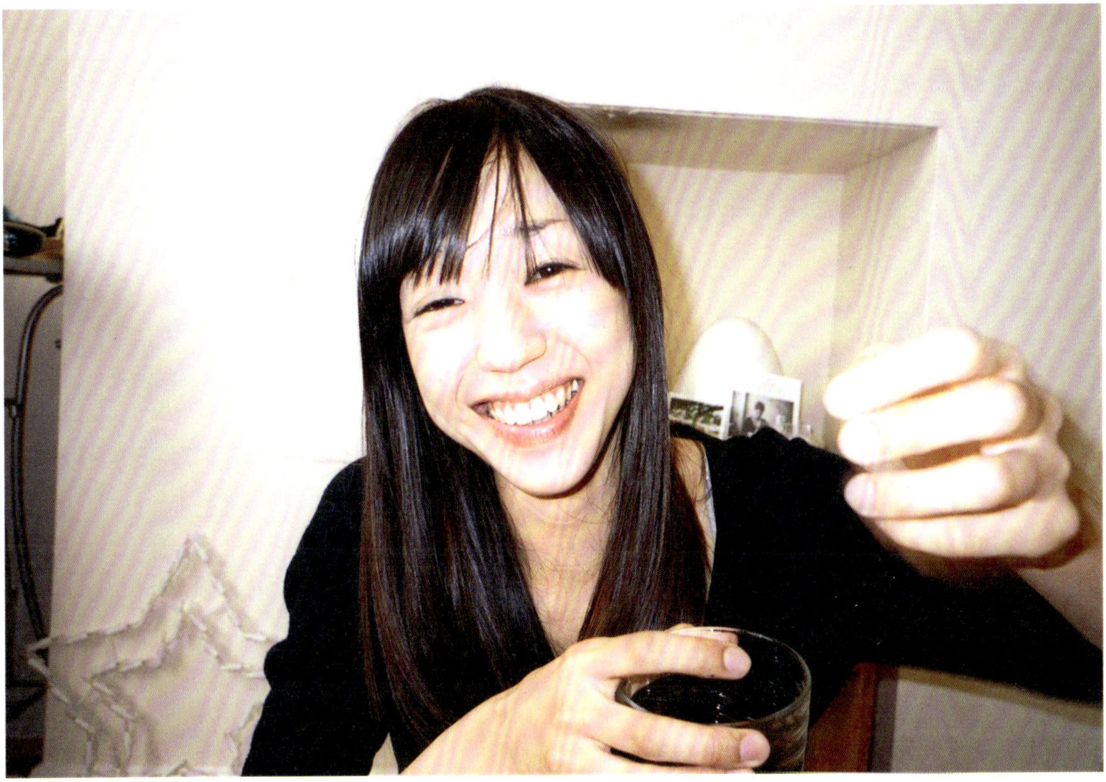

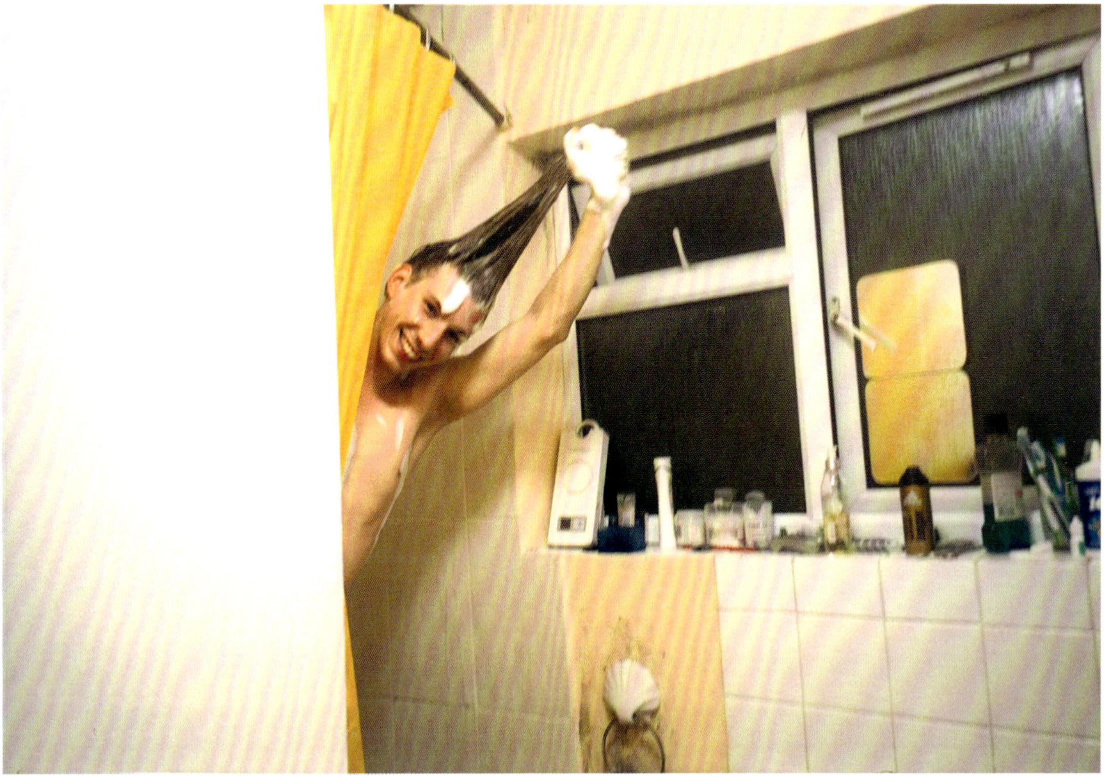

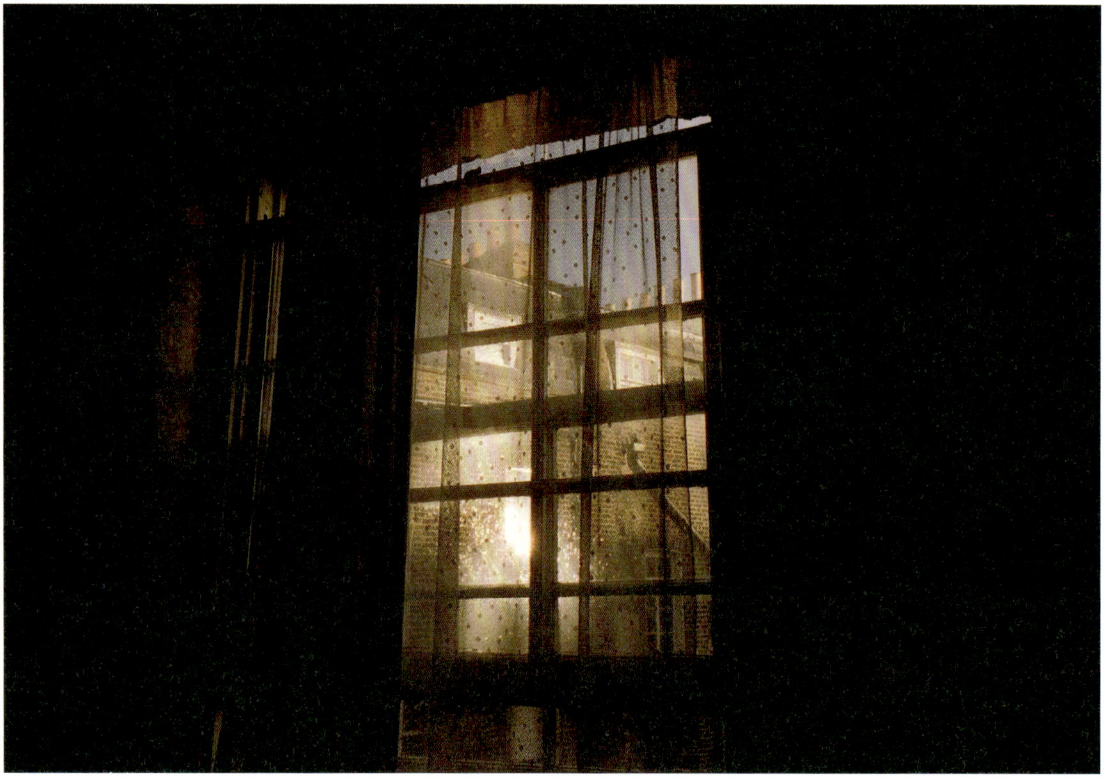

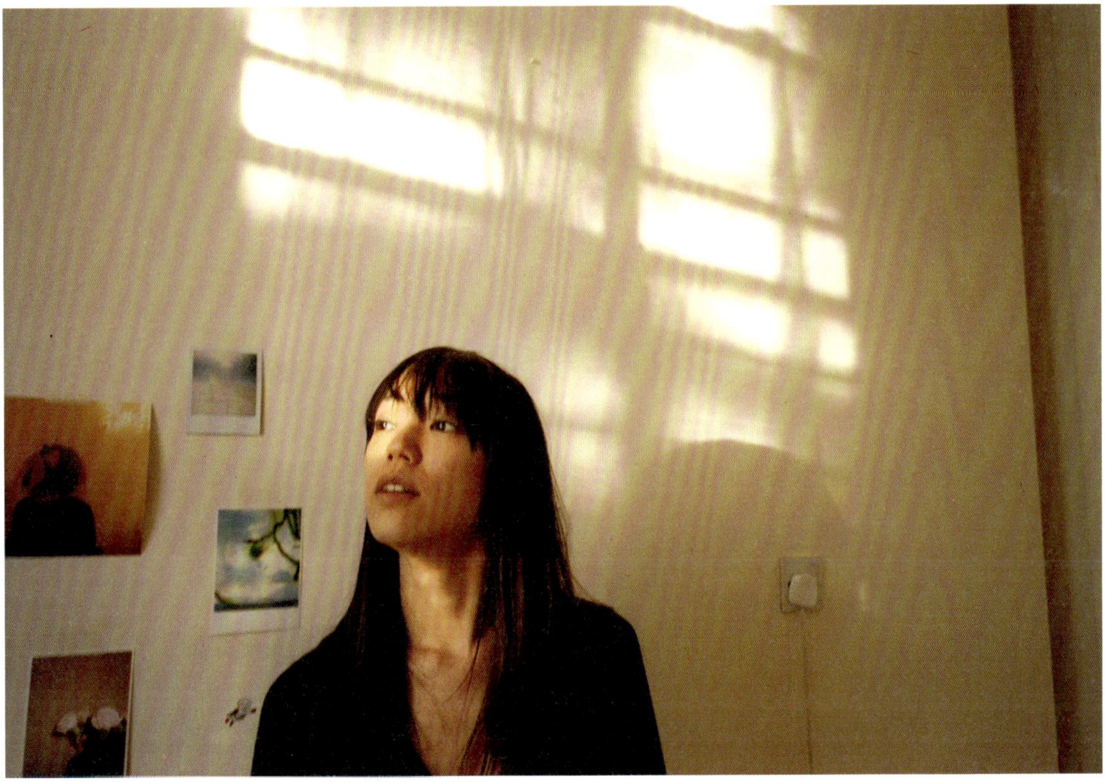

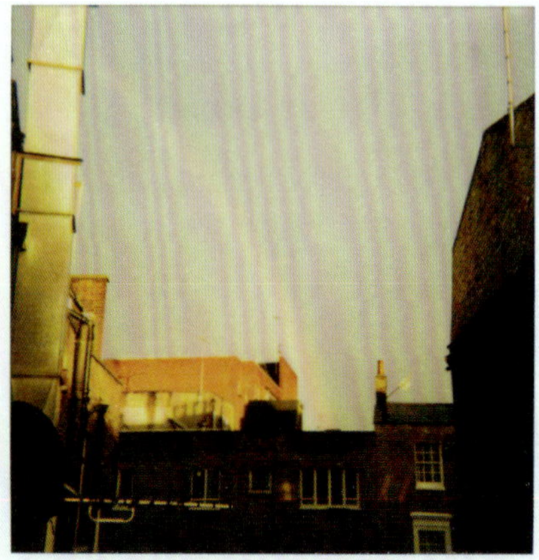

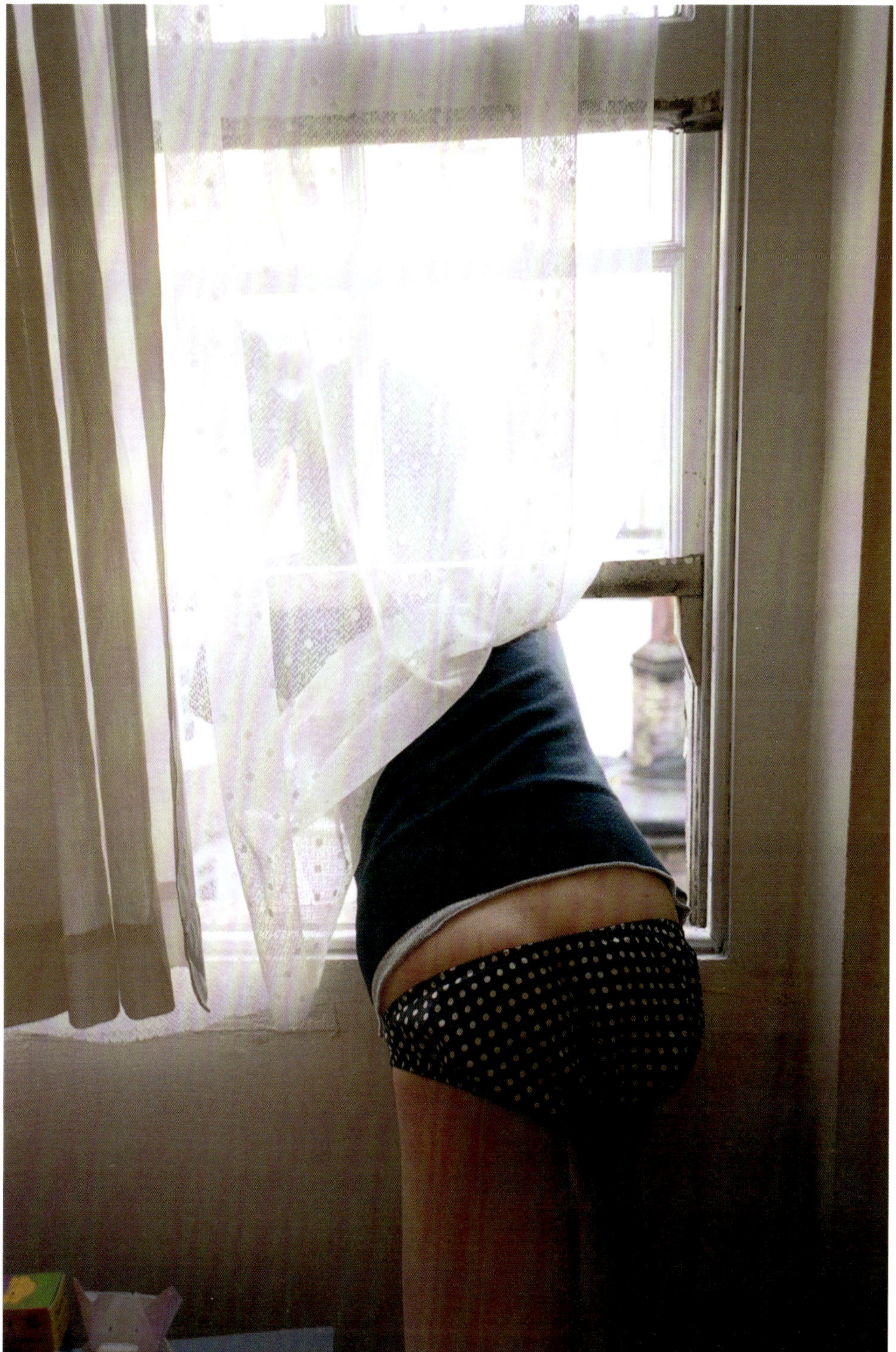

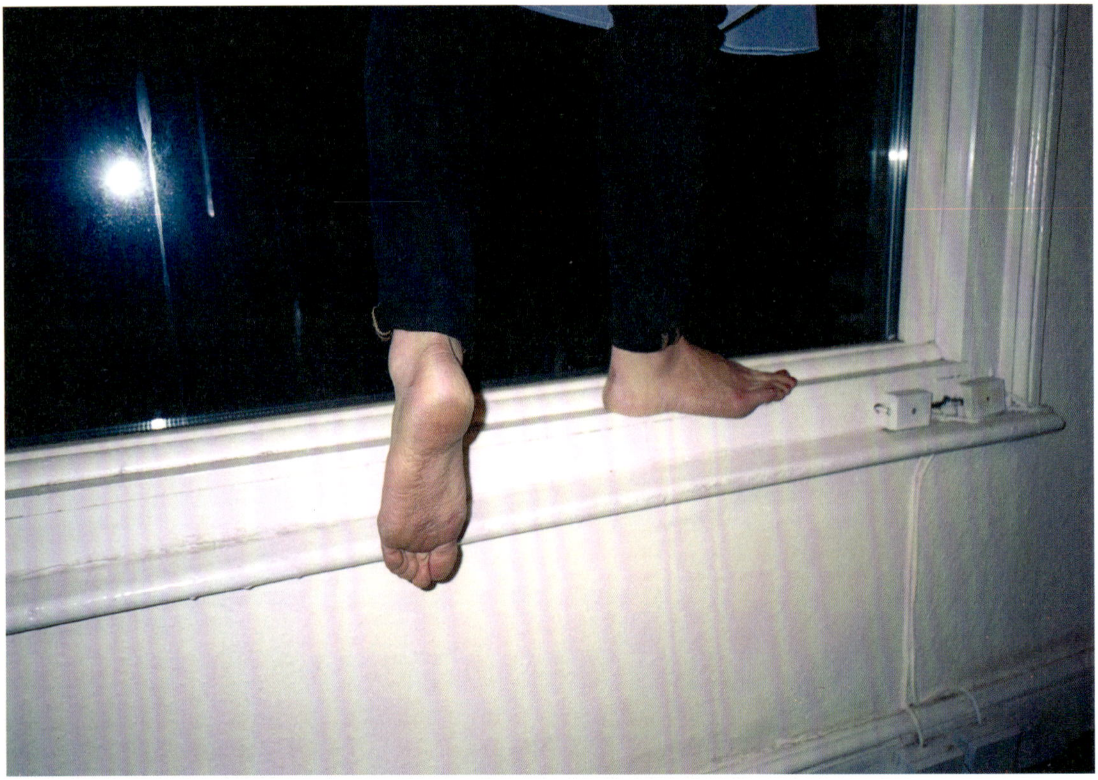

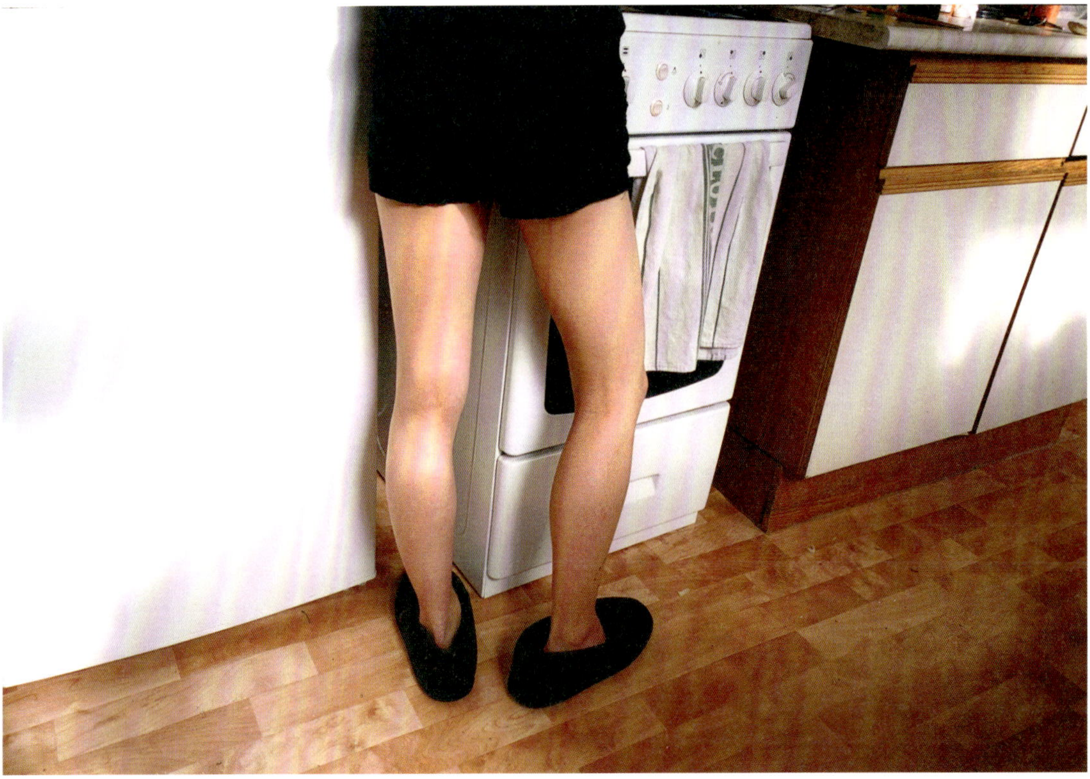

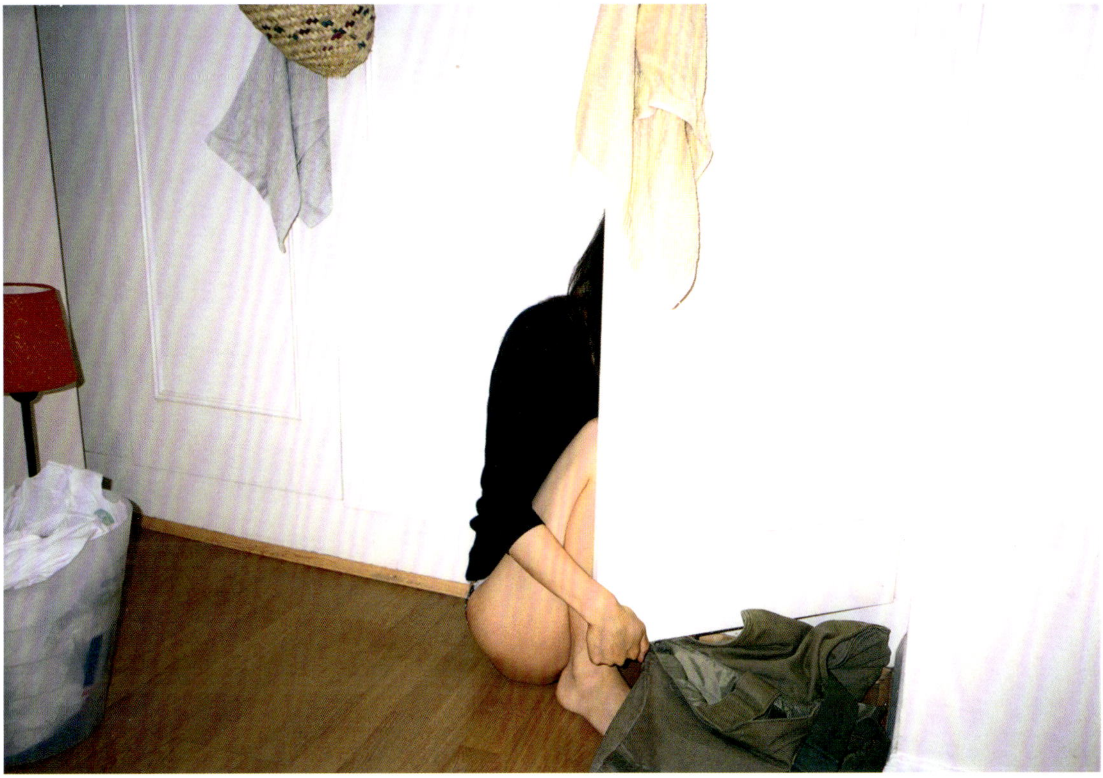

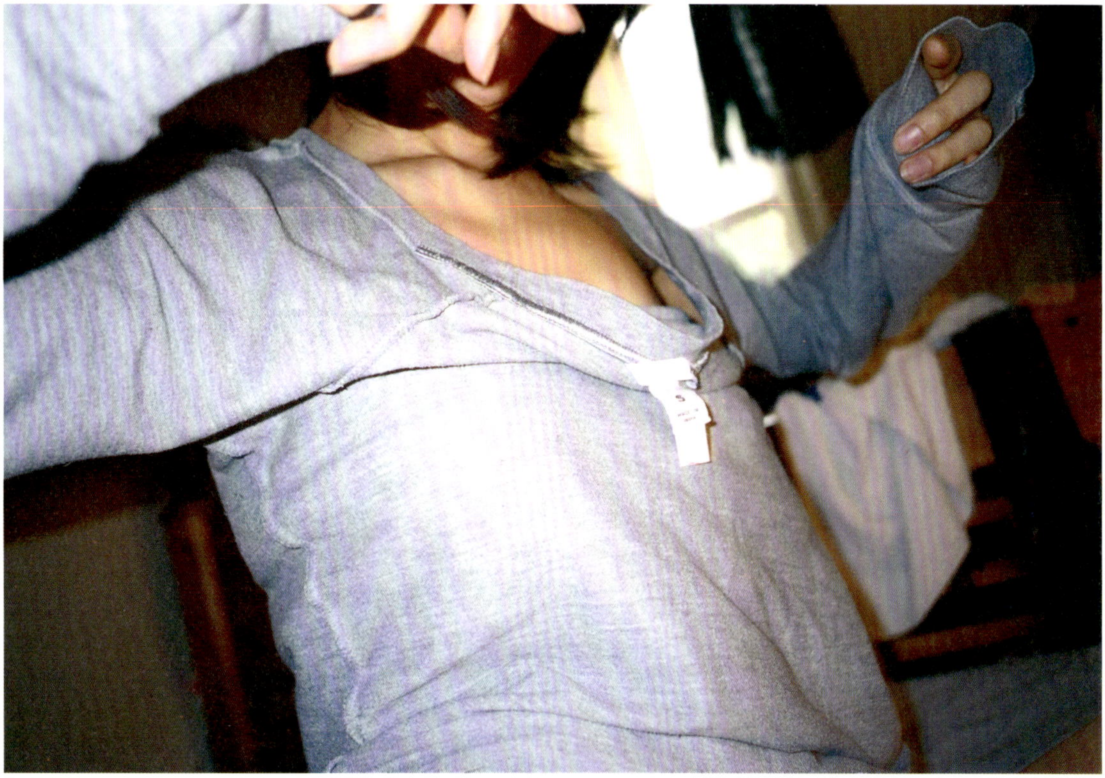

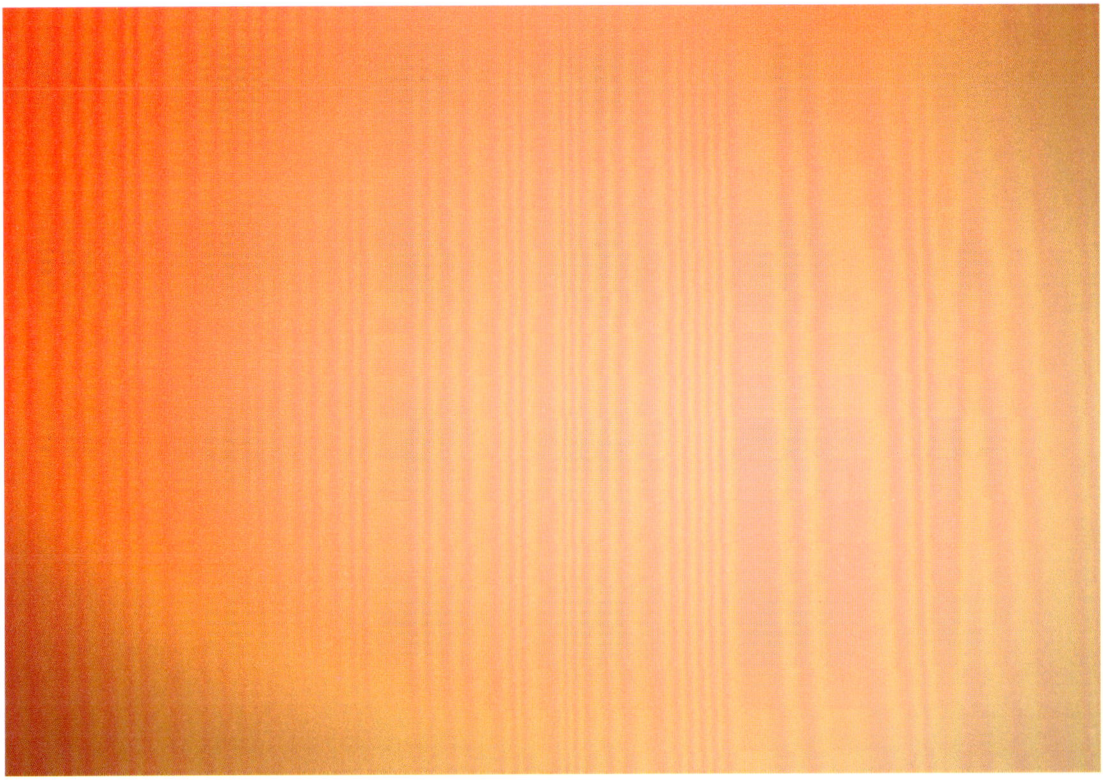

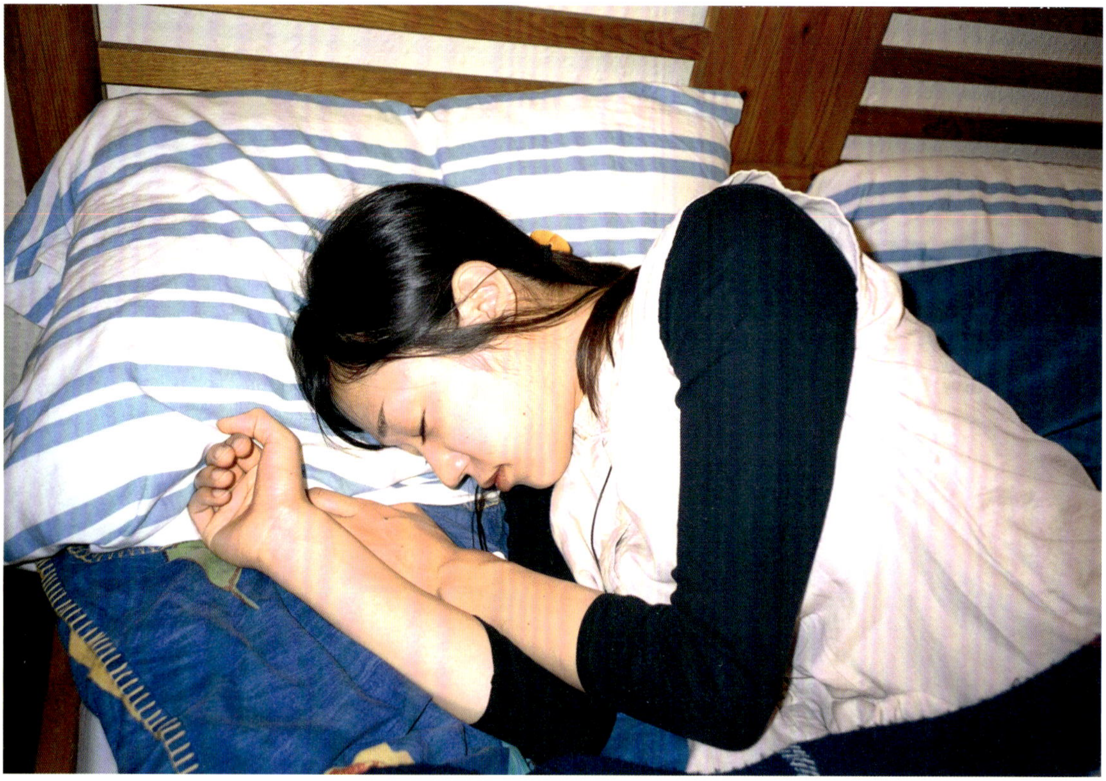

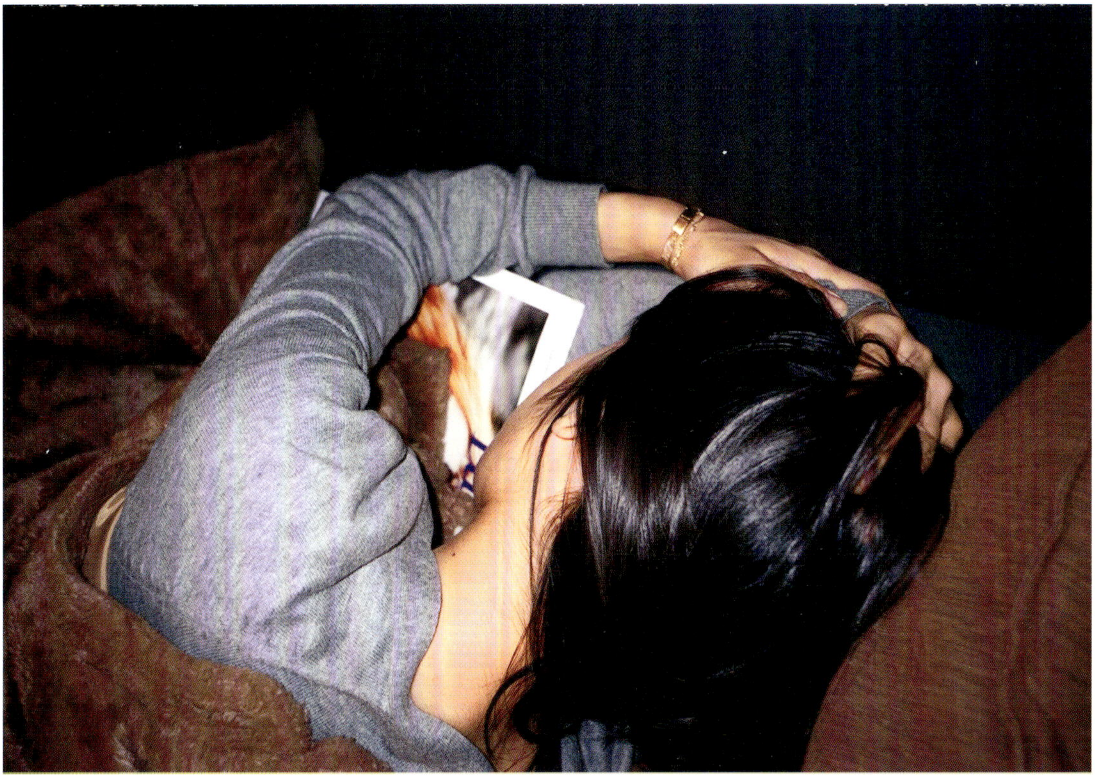

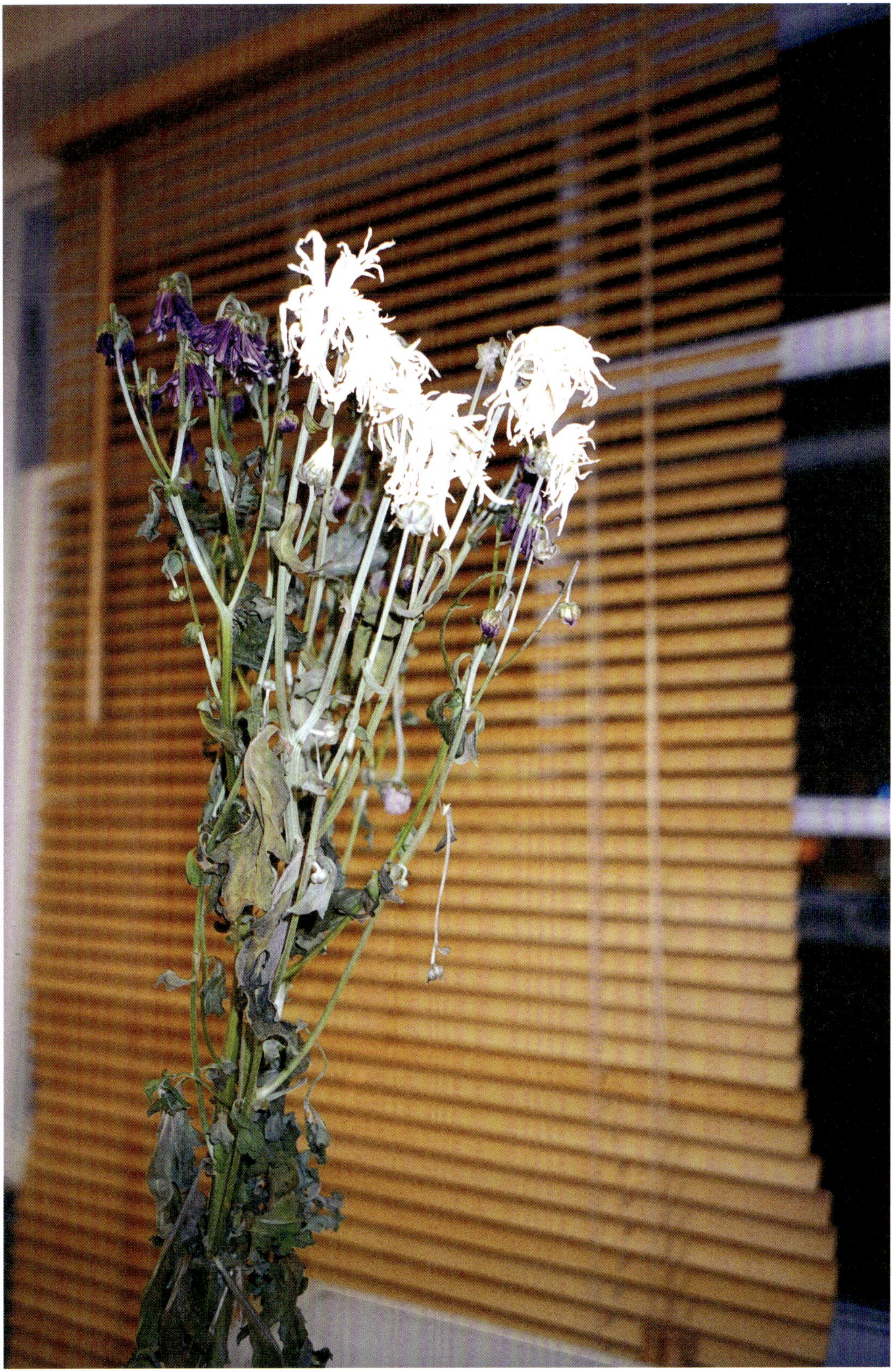

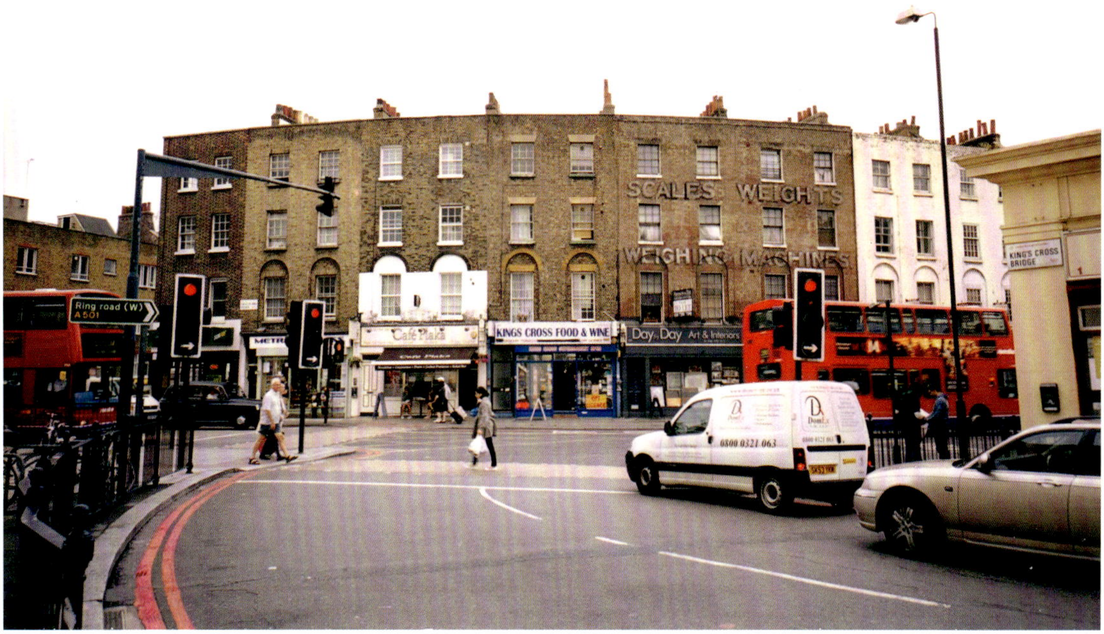
SCALES WEIGHTS
WEIGHING MACHINES
KINGS CROSS FOOD & WINE
Art & Interiors
Ring road (W)
A501
KING'S CROSS
BRIDGE

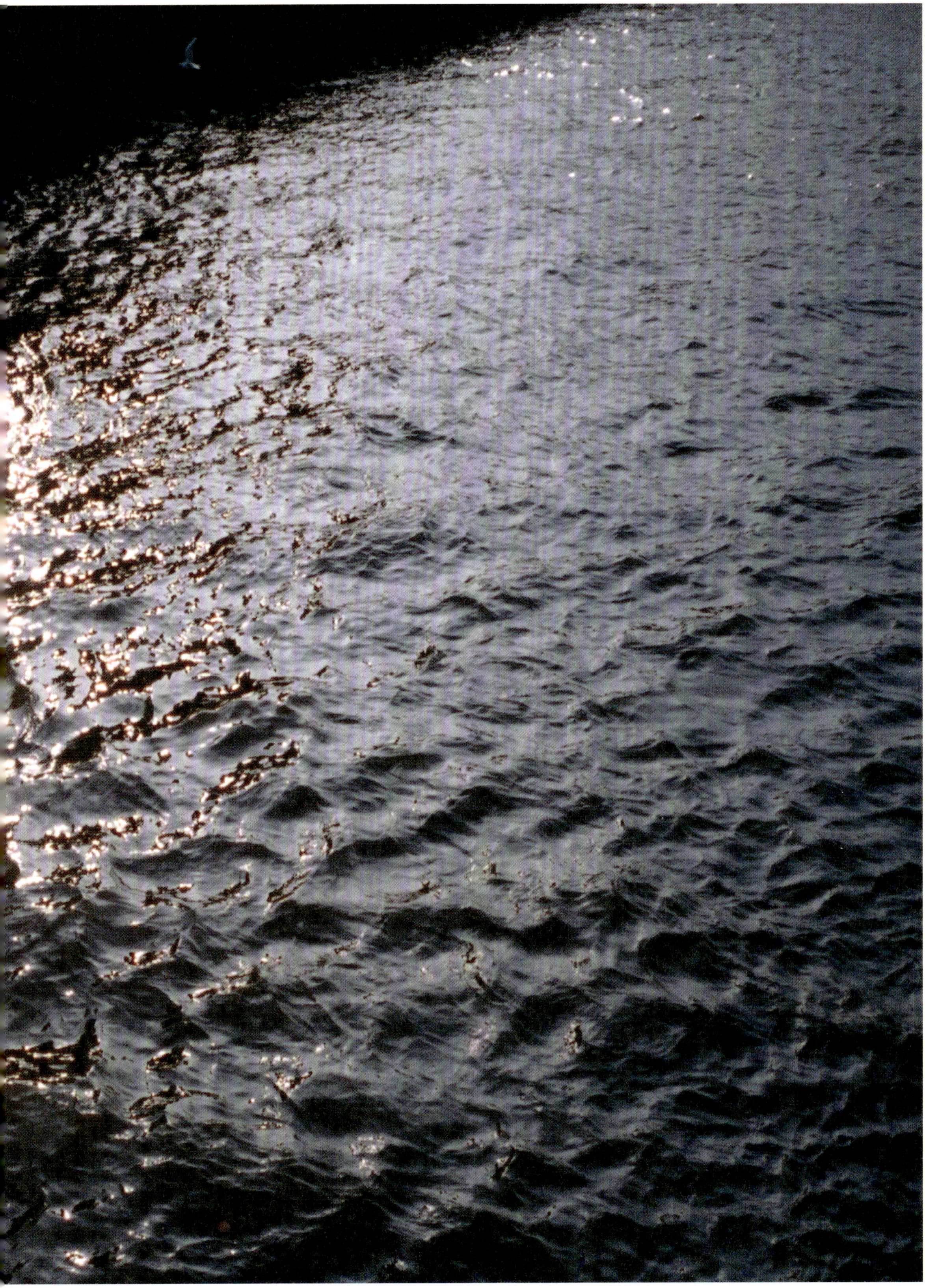

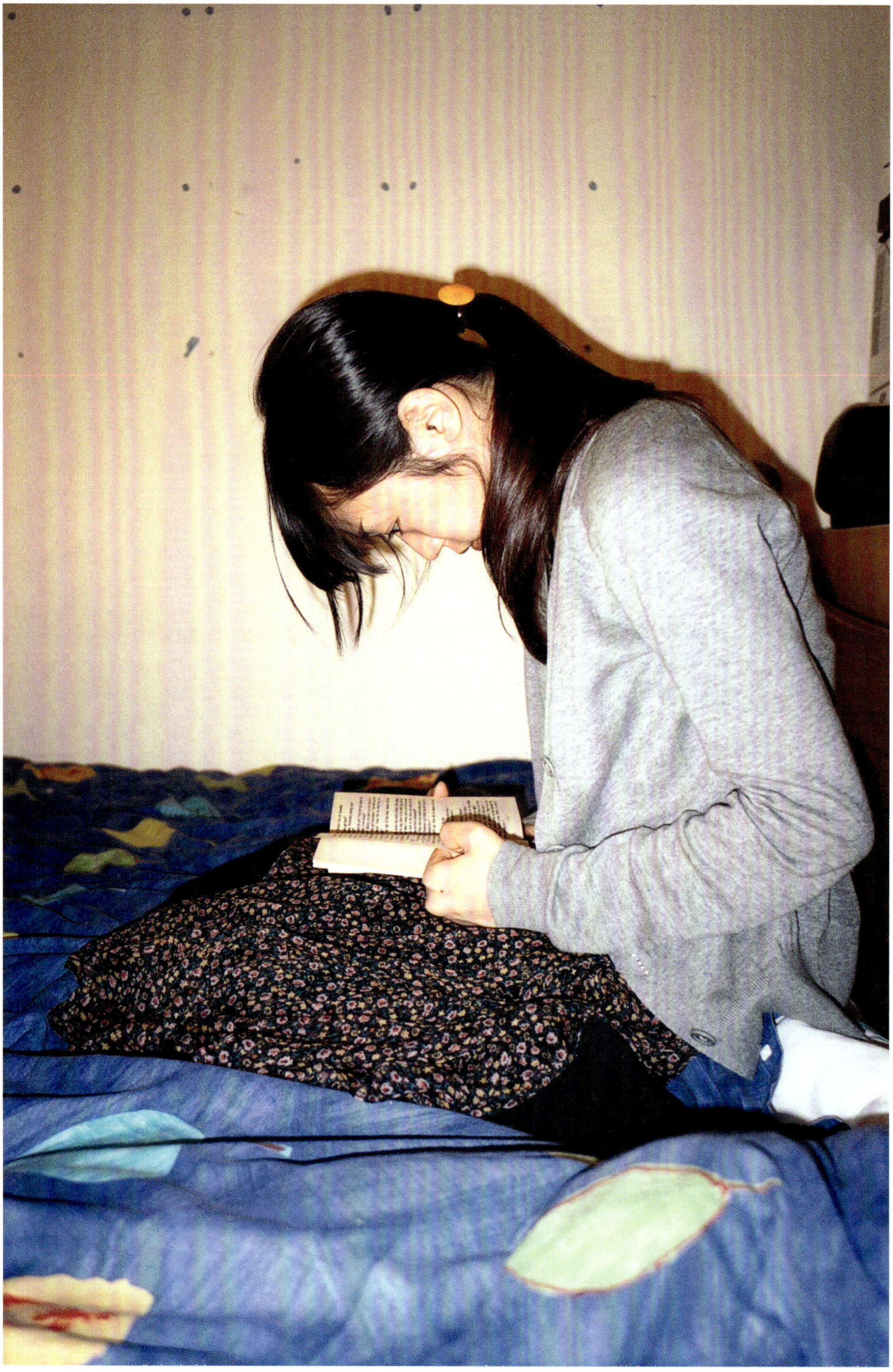

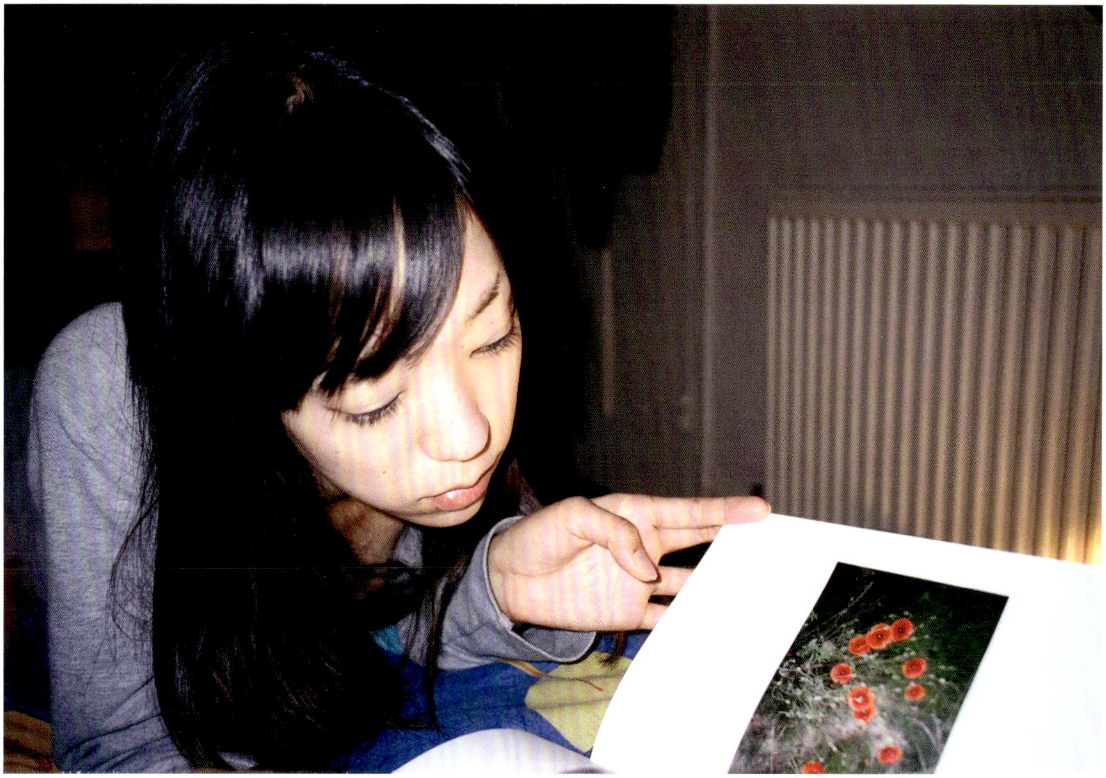

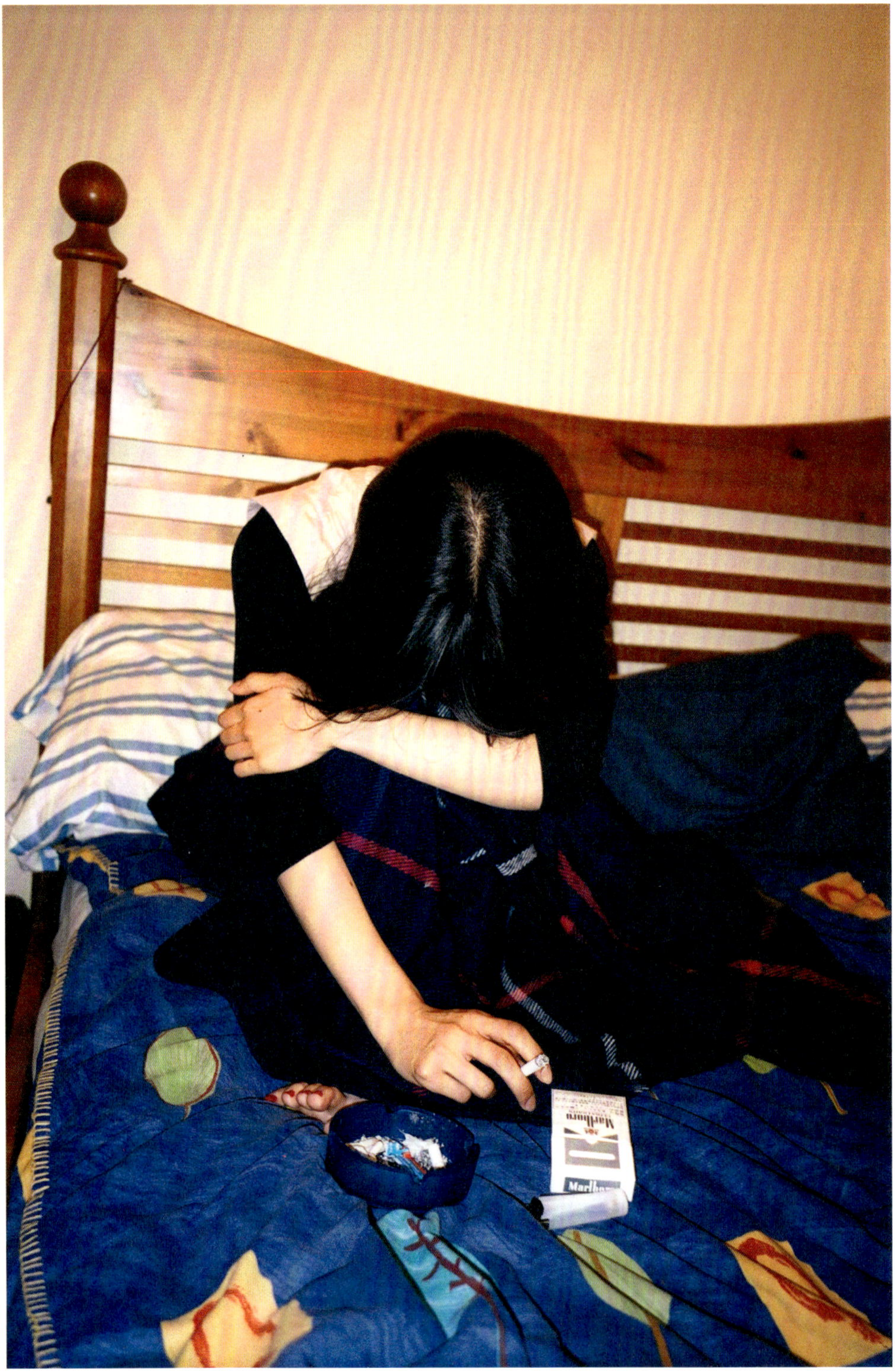

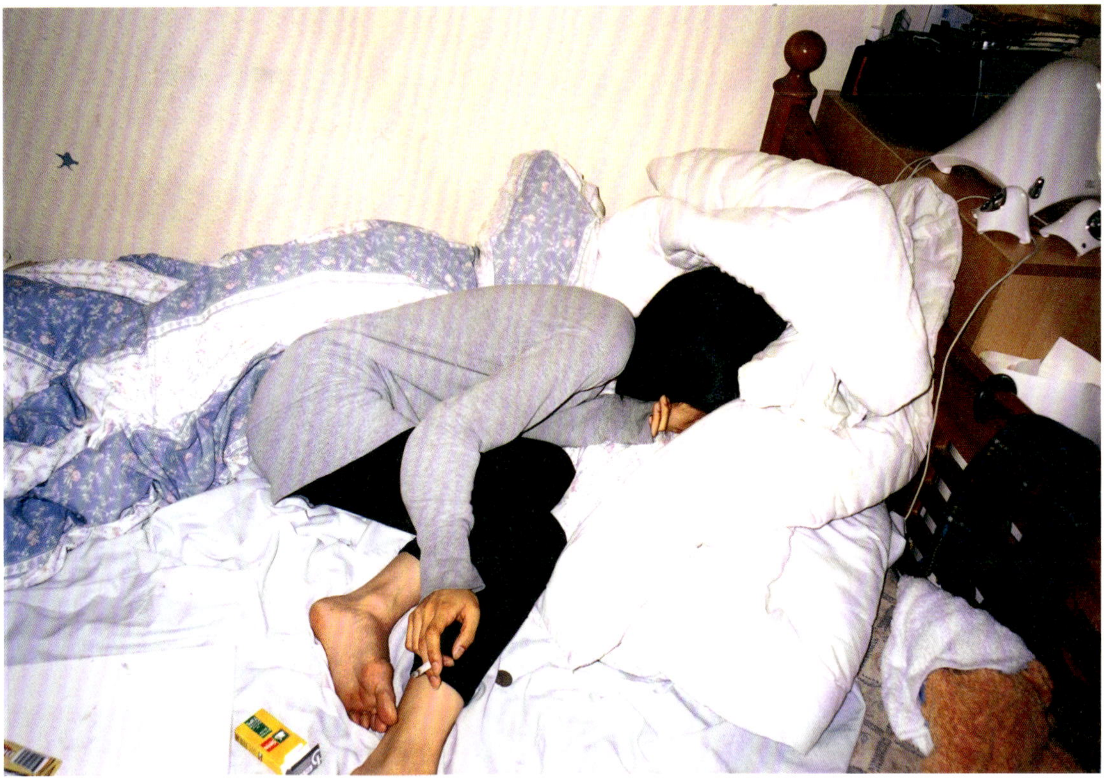

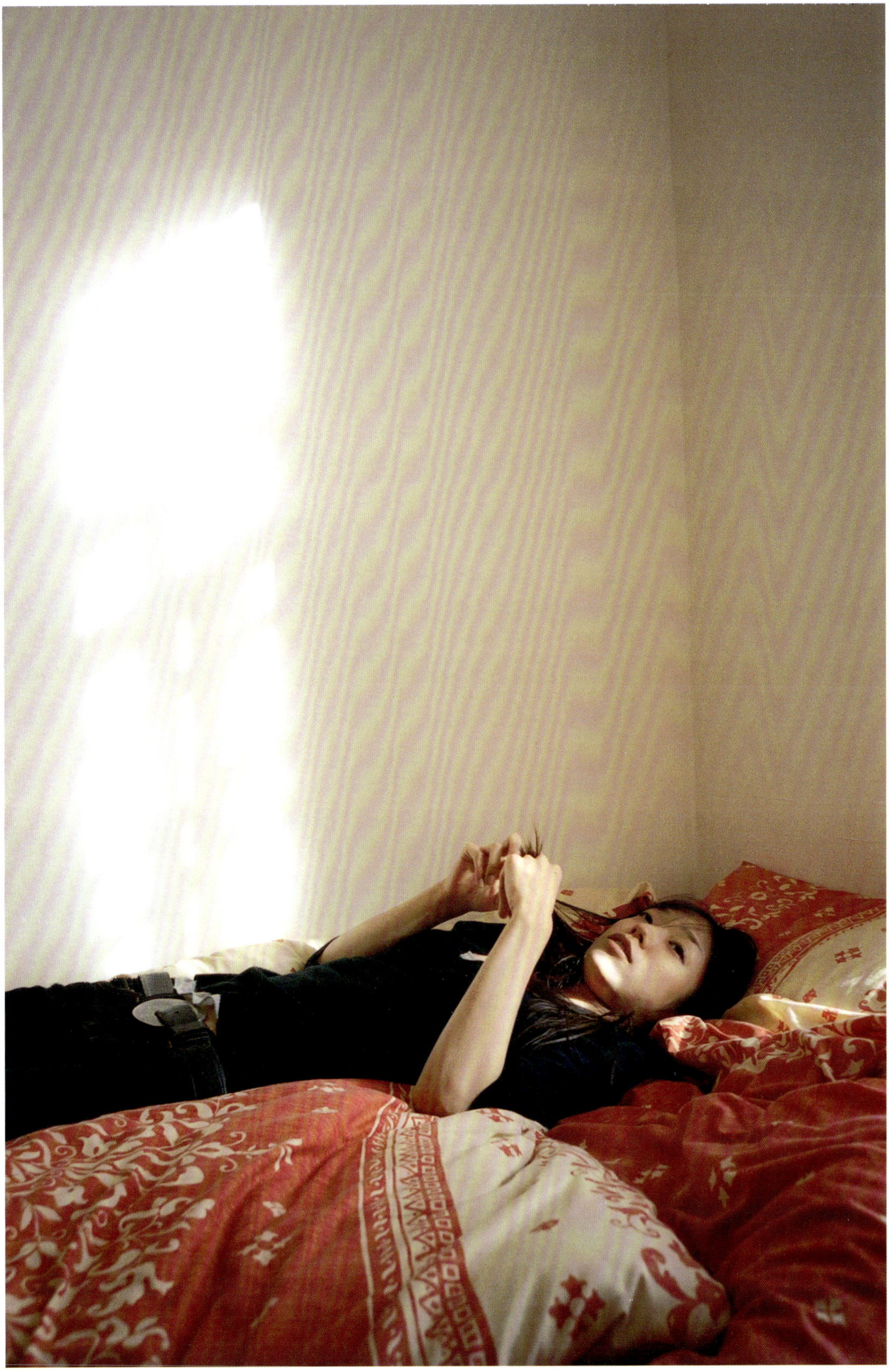

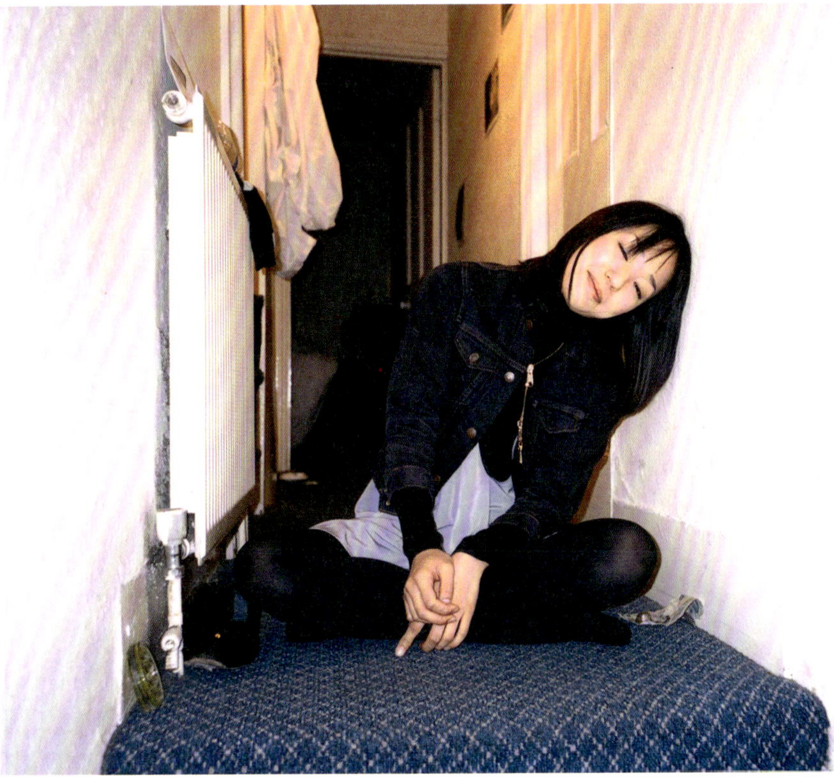

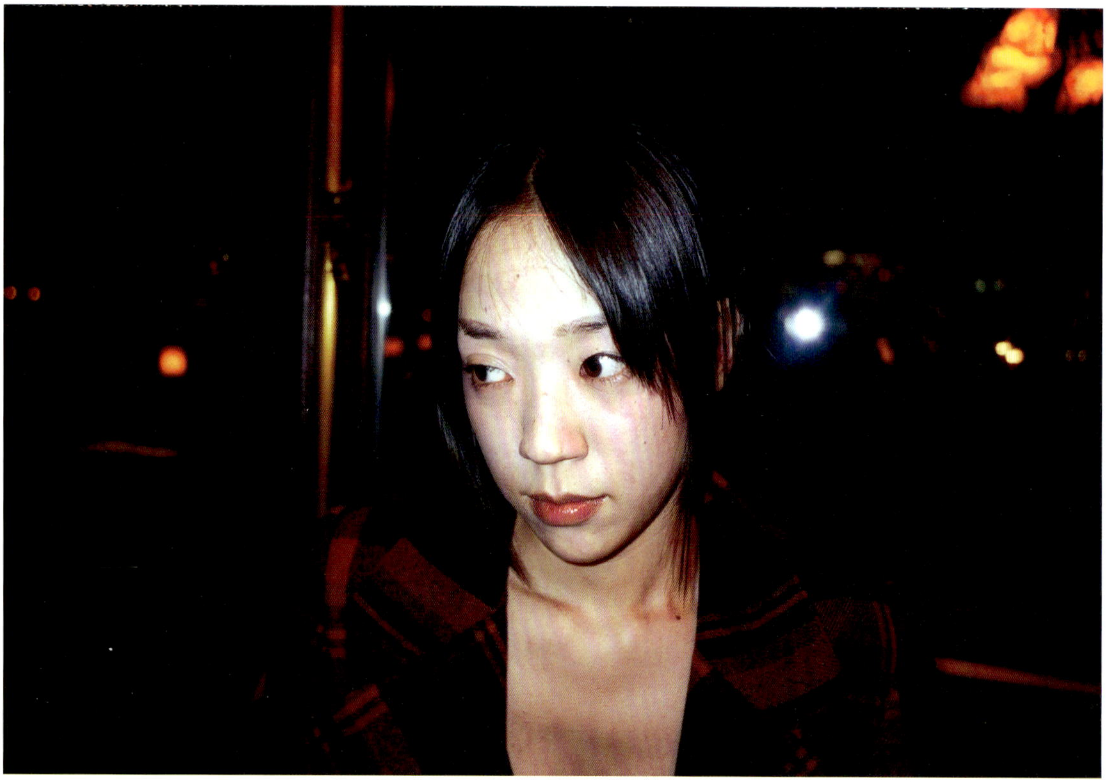

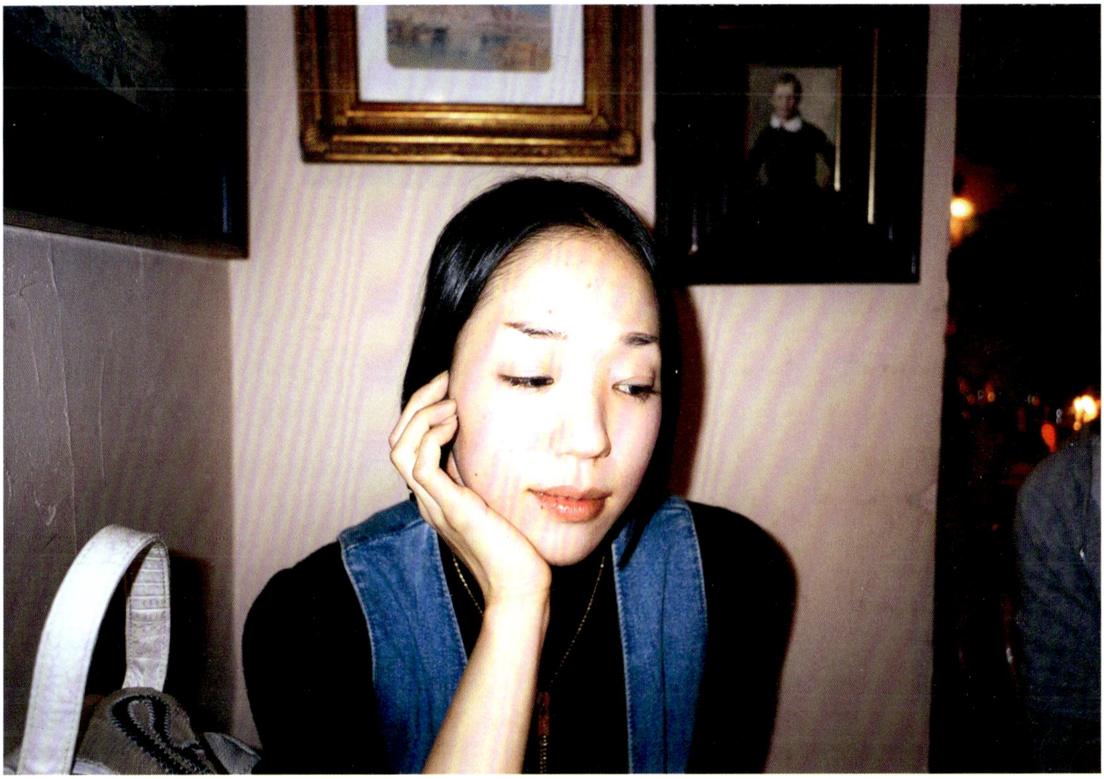

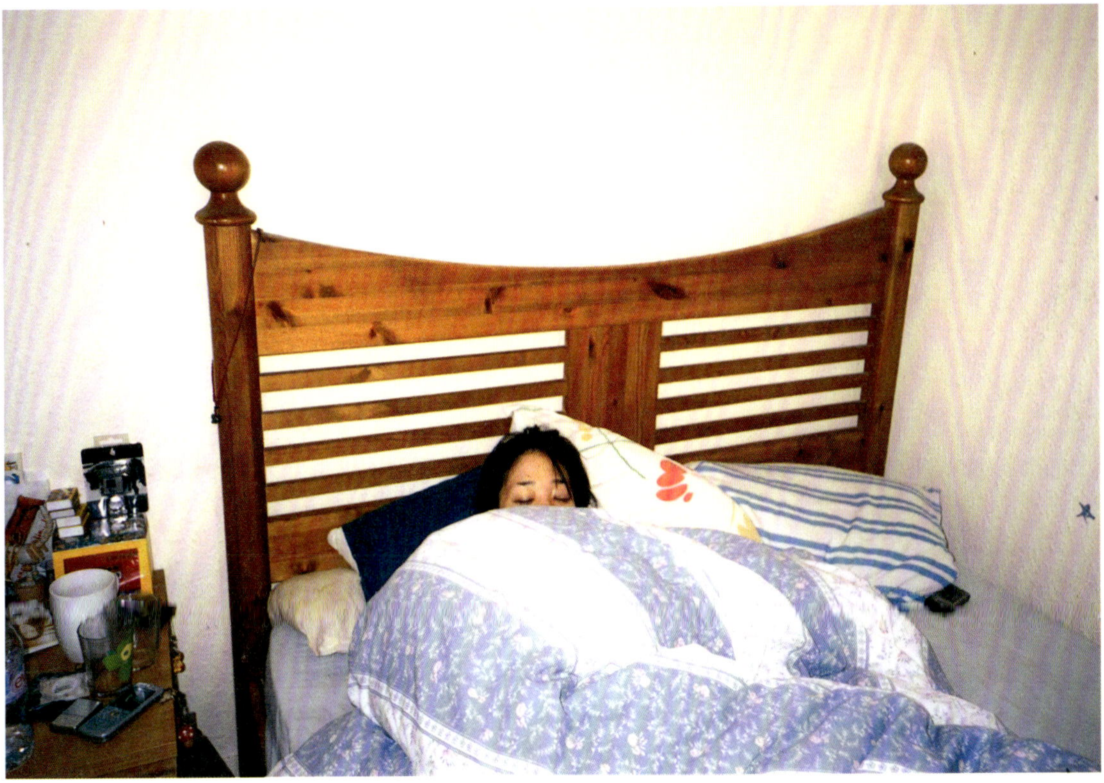

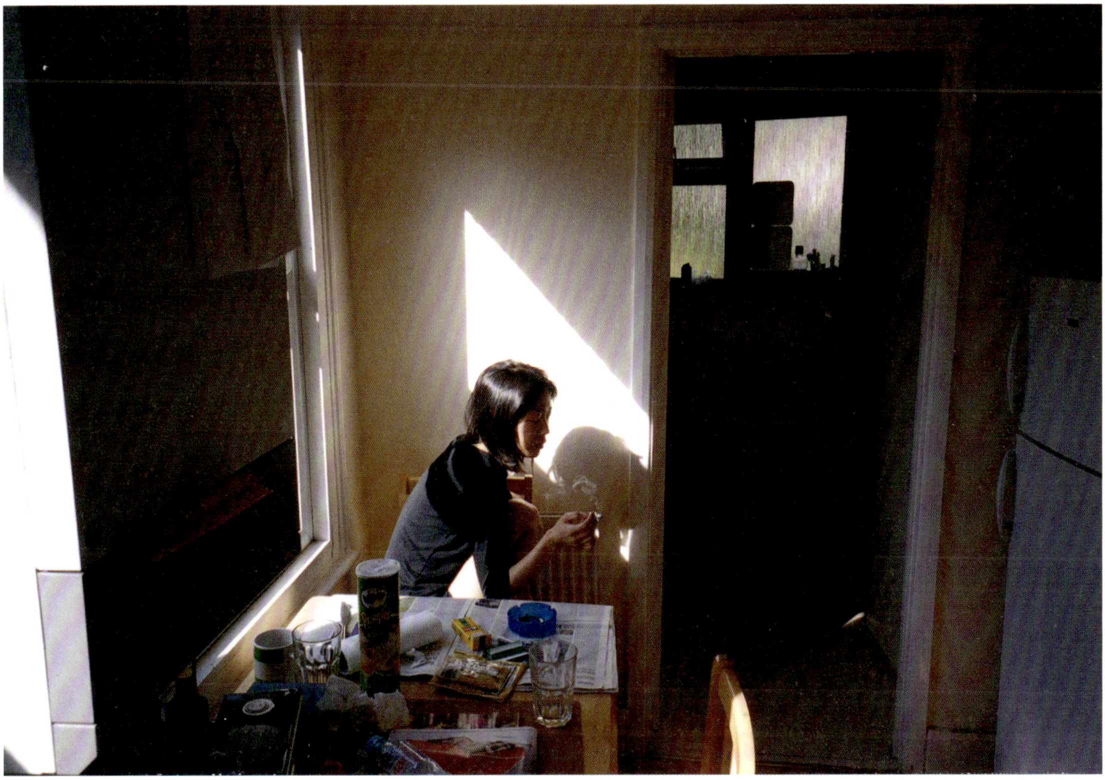

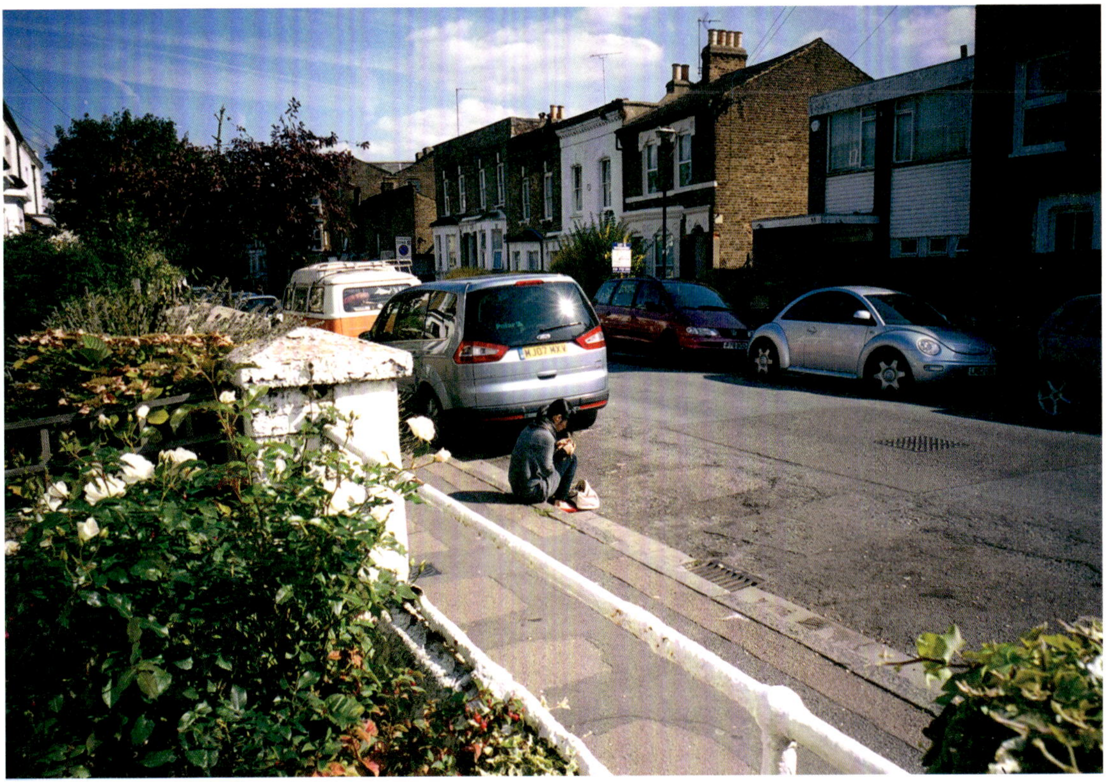

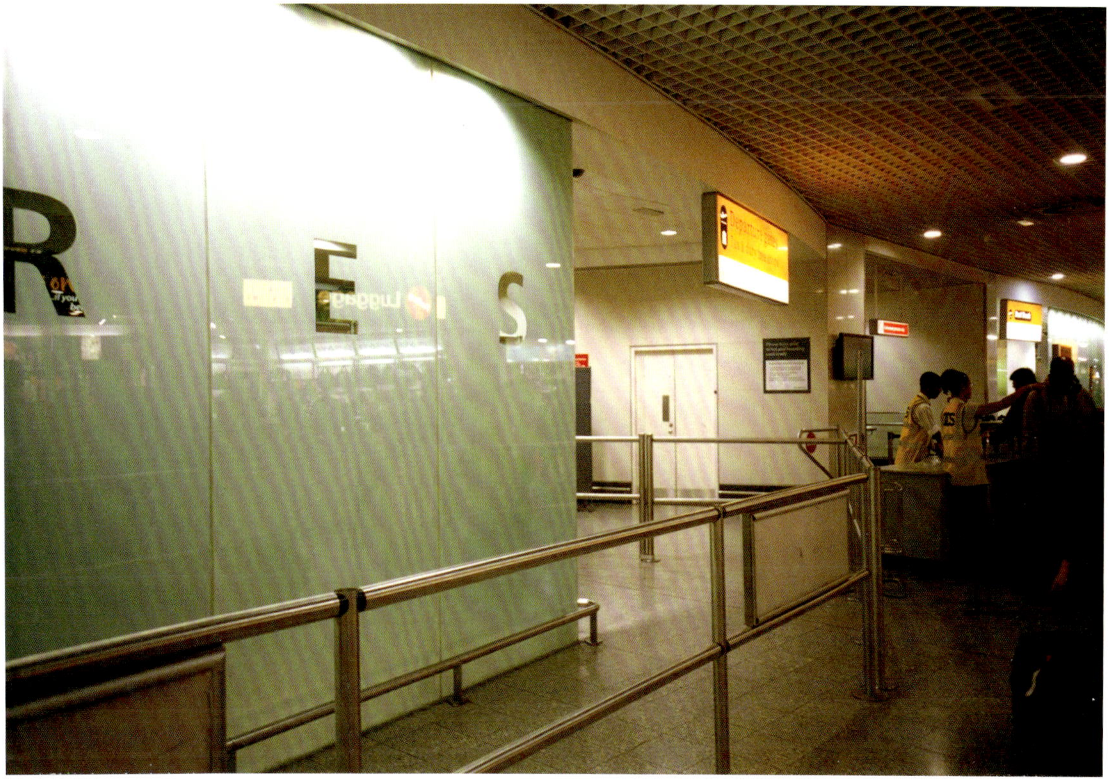
R E S

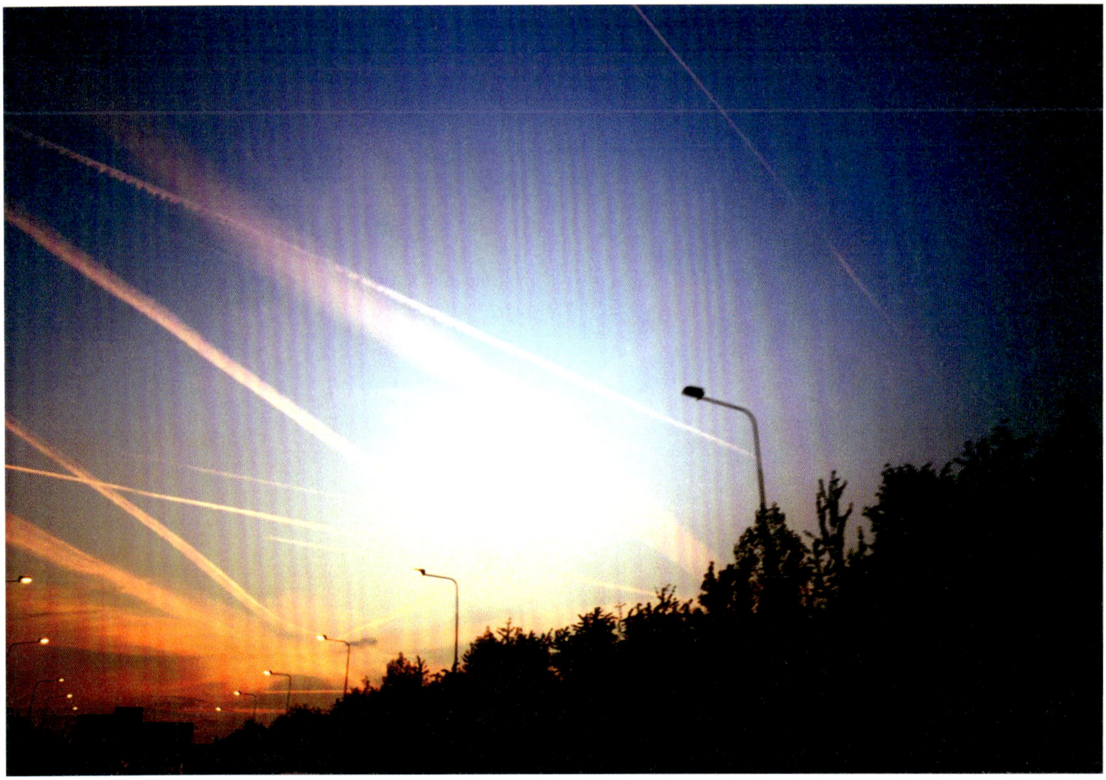

See you soon, Jun

春の半ばを過ぎた頃、ぼくらは出会った。
彼女はひとりで座り、たばこを吸いながら空を見上げていた。

ぼくは彼女の写真を撮りたいと思った。

それから何度か偶然出あうことがあった。
彼女は夜のテムズ川沿いを歩くのがとても好きで、
ぼくはいつしかついて行くようになった。

彼女はペッカムにあるぼくの小さなフラットに越してきて、ぼくと暮らし始めた。
あまり外に出かけるというでもなく、ときどき側に座りながらそれぞれに本を読んだりした。

夏が終わりを迎えた頃、ビザの切れる彼女はロンドンを去らなければいけなくなった。
彼女がヒースローの出国ゲートを歩いていったのを見送ったあと、
ぼくは、ひとり、車で家に戻った。

空がきれいだった。

彼女が最後に見たであろう、イギリスの、とても綺麗な眺めをぼくは想像した。
どれほど彼女を恋しく思うだろうかをその時、実感した。

それ以来、彼女に会っていない。

We met during late spring.
She was sitting alone, smoking a cigarette and gazing at the sky.

I was immediately compelled to photograph her.

We had a few chance meetings.
She enjoyed wandering by the Thames at night.
I started to join her.

She came to live with me in my small flat in Peckham.
We didn't go out much, sometimes we would just read together.

At the end of summer she had to leave London when her visa expired.
After I watched her walk through the departures gate at Heathrow,
I drove home.

The sky was beautiful.

I imagined what a beautiful last view she would have of England.
I realised how much I would miss her.

I haven't seen her since.

See You Soon
またあうひまで

Maxwell Anderson

First published 2010
By Bemojake
www.bemojake.eu
info@bemojake.eu

Edition of 500

Photographs and text: Maxwell Anderson
Additional photographs: Jun Igarashi
Translation: Yuki Kishino
Cover design: Sagar Patel
Production manager: Yi Chiu Chen

With thanks to:
Jun Igarashi, Yuki Kishino, Sagar Patel,
Yi Chiu Chen, Lucy Soutter, Edward Dimsdale,
Chris Boot, Tony White, Reuben Le Prevost,
Melanie Vogel, Einar Hansen, Duncan Whyte,
Caitlin Duennebier, Ting Shu, Tomomi Sayuda,
Suk Ju Ryu, Yuri Sawa, Ai Mishiro, Aki Tsujimoto,
Tsukasa Nishimura.

A CIP catalogue record for this book is
available from the British Library.

Printed in Taiwan by Mr.Zen

ISBN: 978-0-9562470-1-8

Bemojake

Sport
Illustra

STARS OF S

KYLIAN MBAPPÉ

FOOTBALL ICON

by Ryan G. Van Cleave

raintree
a Capstone company — publishers for children

Raintree is an imprint of Capstone Global Library Limited, a company incorporated in England and Wales having its registered office at 264 Banbury Road, Oxford, OX2 7DY – Registered company number: 6695582

www.raintree.co.uk
myorders@raintree.co.uk

Editorial credits
Edited by Christianne Jones
Designed by Jaime Willems
Media Research by Jo Miller and Svetlana Zhurkin
Production by Whitney Schaefer
Originated by Capstone Global Library Ltd

ISBN 978 1 3982 5949 2

British Library Cataloguing in Publication Data
A full catalogue record for this book is available from the British Library.

Acknowledgements
We would like to thank the following for permission to reproduce photographs: Alamy: Abaca Press/Henri Szwarc, 7, Abaca Press/Jerome Domine, 21, Abaca Press/Laurent Zabulon, 19, DPPI Media/Stephane Allman, 5, Xinhua/Cao Can, 15; Associated Press: Thibault Camus, cover, 8; Getty Images: Oisin Keniry, 25; Newscom: MAXPPP/Leon Tanguy, 13, Xinhua News Agency/Gao Jing, 23, ZUMA Press/Panoramic, 10, 27, 28; Shutterstock: August_0802, 17, Christian Bertrand, 26, EFKS, 1, Influential Photography, 11, Victor Velter, 16

Source Notes
Page 9, "Kylian would always think about football . . ." John Bennett, "Kylian Mbappé: How France World Cup star rose to prominence", BBV World Service Sport, 30 June 2018, www.bbc.co.uk/sport/football/44669497. Accessed June 2023.
Page 9, "I'm going to play. . ." Jeremy Patrelle, "10 things we learned about Kylian Mbappé in the L'Quipe documentary", *GQ France*, 7 November 2017, www.gqmagazine.fr/lifestyle/sport/articles/10-trucs-que-lon-a-appris-sur-kylian-mbappe-dans-le-docu-kylian-hors-normes-de-lequipe-enquete/57616. Accessed June 2023.
Page 12, "It was hard for me to be . . ." "Kylian Mbappé: Paris St-Germain forward wants his charity to help kids live their dream", BBC, 22 January, 2020, www.bbc.co.uk/newsround/51187358. Accessed June 2023.
Page 18, "We will return . . ." Sam Blitz, "Kylian Mbappé: France star well-laced to become the best player on the planet after World Cup heroics", Sky Sports, 20 December 2023, www.skysports.com/football/news/11095/12771383/kylian-mbappe-france-star-well-placed-to-become-the-best-player-on-the-planet-after-world-cup-final-heroics. Accessed June 2023.
Page 22, "It doesn't change my life . . ." Ken Browne, "Kylian Mbappé: 12 things you may not know about France's football star", Olympics.com, 25 April 2023, https://olympics.com/en/news/kylian-mbappe-tokyo-olympics-12-fun-facts. Accessed June 2023.
Page 27, "Mbappé is the future and the present . . ." The Esquire Editors, "What Football Legends Have to Say About Kylian Mbappé", *Esquire*, 2 June 2 2021, www.esquire.com/uk/culture/a36600159/what-football-legends-have-to-say-about-kylian-mbappe. Accessed June 2023.
Page 28, "I am aware of the risk. . ." Jason Burt, "Grounded Kylian Mbappe will go all the way to the very top of the game", *The Telegraph*, 2 July 2018, www.telegraph.co.uk/world-cup/2018/07/02/grounded-kylian-mbappe-will-go-way-top-game. Accessed June 2023.

Printed and bound in India.

CONTENTS

Words in **BOLD** are in the glossary.

WORLD CUP DREAMS COME TRUE

At the age of 19, Kylian Mbappé was playing for the French national team in the biggest football tournament in the world. This was the 2018 FIFA World Cup in Russia. The tournament is played every four years.

The score was 0–0, despite both teams launching shot after shot. Then, 34 minutes into the game, a French teammate **dribbled** up the pitch and tried to score. The shot was **deflected**. Mbappé saw his chance. He charged in and smashed the ball into the net.

GOAL!

The crowd went wild! Mbappé became the youngest player to score in a World Cup final. The team went on to beat Croatia and win the World Cup.

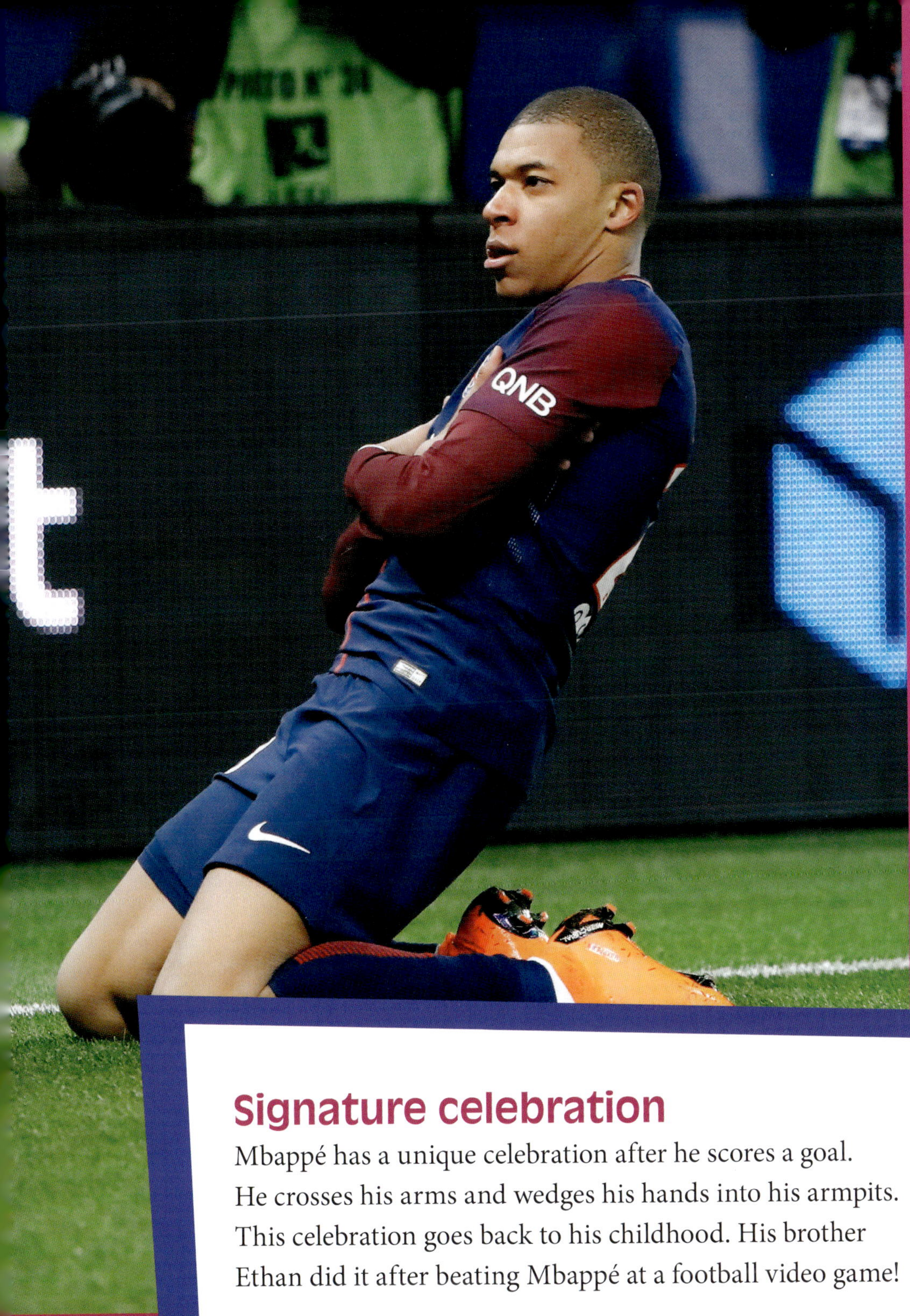

Signature celebration

Mbappé has a unique celebration after he scores a goal. He crosses his arms and wedges his hands into his armpits. This celebration goes back to his childhood. His brother Ethan did it after beating Mbappé at a football video game!

CHAPTER ONE

A STAR IN THE MAKING

Kylian Mbappé Lottin was born in Paris, France, on 20 December 1998. He grew up in Bondy, an area of Paris. His father, Wilfried, was a footballer and coach. His mother, Fayza, was a former professional handball player. They created a supportive and sport-loving environment for Mbappé and his two brothers.

All three boys loved football from the start. Mbappé's adopted older brother, Jirès Kembo Ekoko, was already playing football at a high level. Mbappé and his younger brother, Ethan, showed exceptional ability too.

Because their father was first a player and later a coach, the boys grew up around football. Mbappé followed his father everywhere. He took part in training sessions when he was just 3 years old.

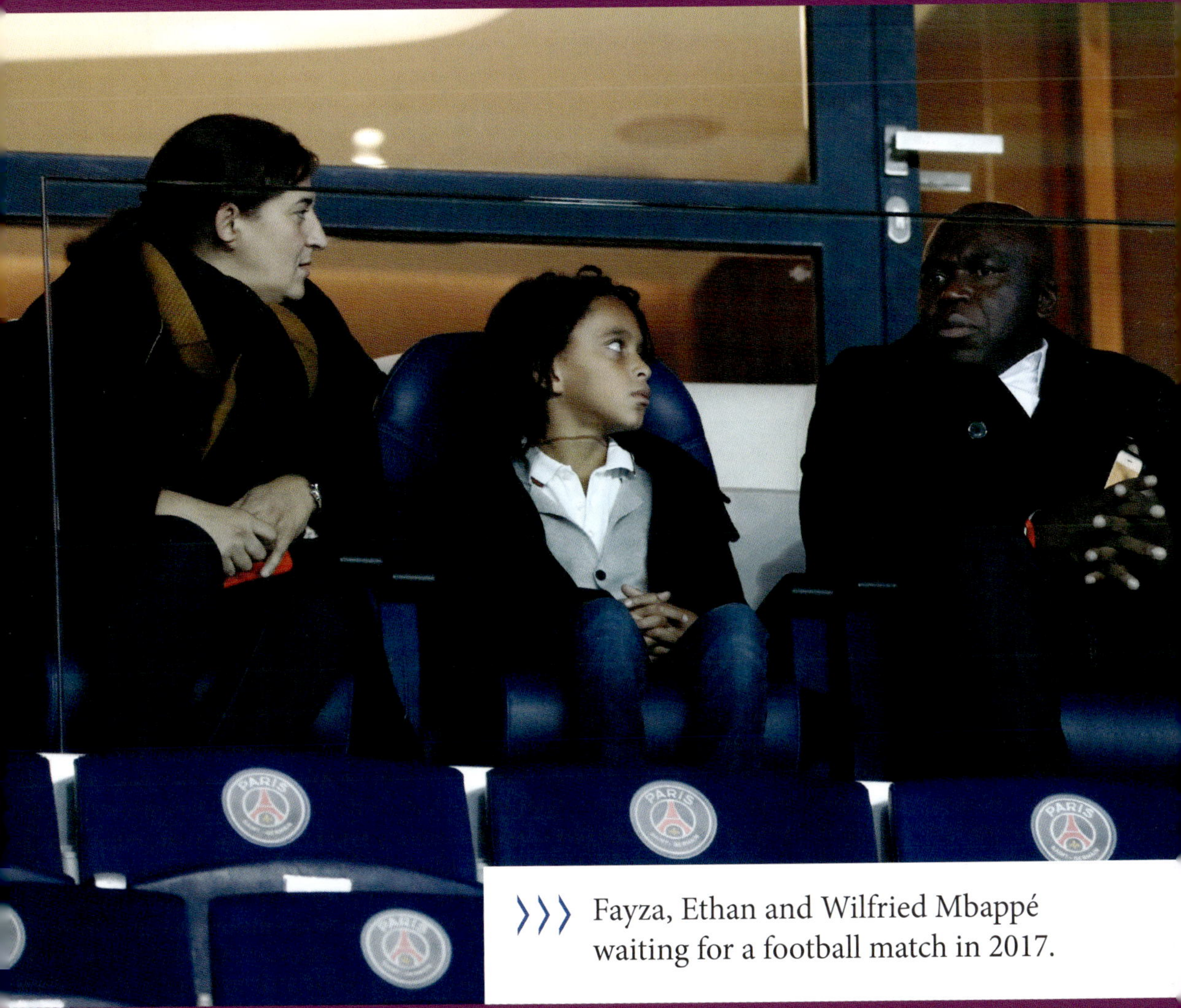

››› Fayza, Ethan and Wilfried Mbappé waiting for a football match in 2017.

When he was 6 years old, Mbappé joined AS Bondy. It was his local football team. His father was the coach. Mbappé's speed and ability in scoring goals set him apart from others. He quickly became an outstanding player.

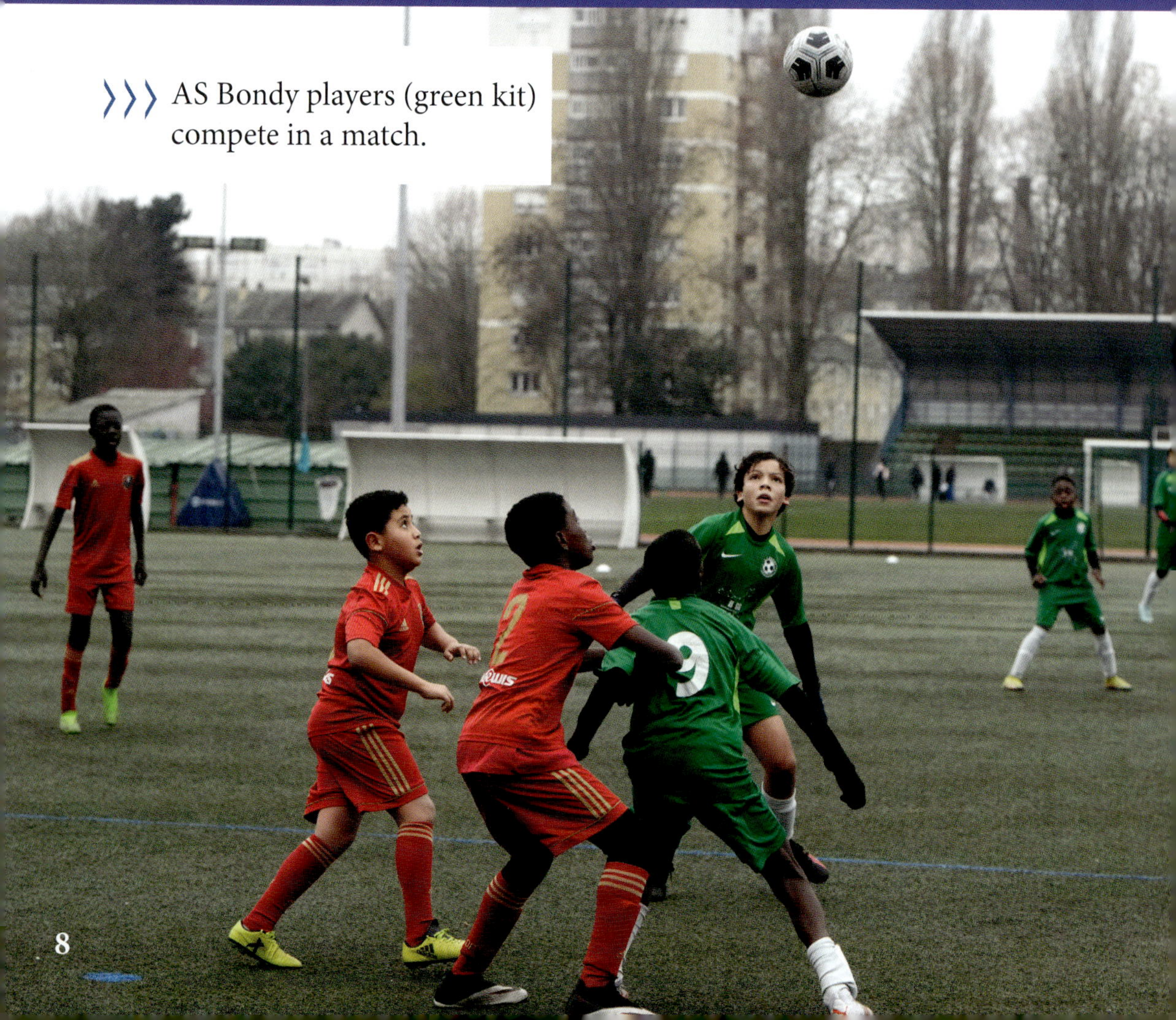

AS Bondy players (green kit) compete in a match.

Antonio Riccardi, who coached the AS Bondy under-13 team, said, "Kylian would always think about football, always talk about football, always watch football – and if he wasn't doing that he'd be playing football games on the PlayStation."

Mbappé also played football with his friends in the Bondy streets. He couldn't get enough! He had big dreams of becoming a professional footballer. "I'm going to play in the French team," he told everyone. "I'm going to play in the World Cup for France."

Some people laughed when he said that. They weren't laughing for long.

FACT

Between the ages of 6 and 11, Mbappé studied music at a centre for the performing arts. He learned to sing and play the flute.

CHAPTER TWO

RISING THROUGH THE RANKS

Mbappé continued to wow coaches, crowds and **opponents**. In 2011, he enrolled at the INF Clairefontaine. It was a special school for top footballers.

In 2013, 14-year-old Mbappé joined the AS Monaco youth academy. He continued to develop his football skills.

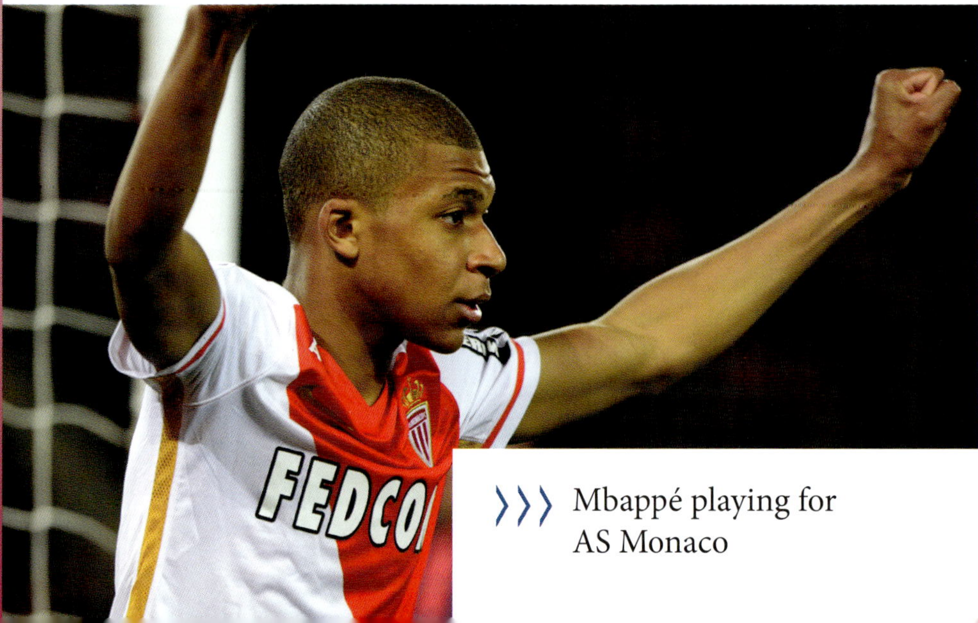

››› Mbappé playing for AS Monaco

››› Mbappé plays in a 2017 game in Paris.

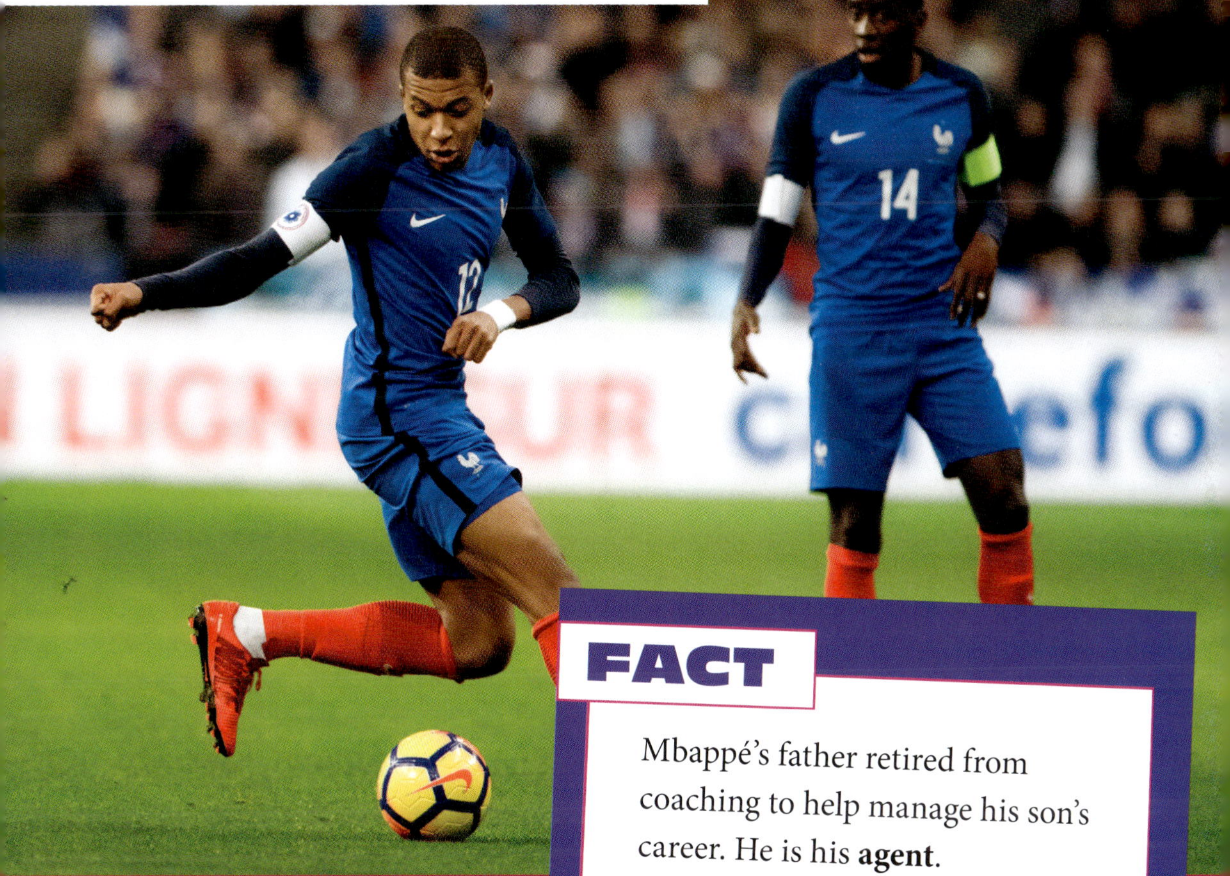

FACT

Mbappé's father retired from coaching to help manage his son's career. He is his **agent**.

Two years later, he made his professional **debut** with the club. With his help, AS Monaco won the French Ligue 1 title in the 2016–2017 season. His performance on the pitch didn't go unnoticed. Mbappé received the Golden Boy award in 2017 as the best under-21 player in Europe.

Mbappé's dazzling play also drew the attention of Paris Saint-Germain (PSG). It is one of the top football clubs in Europe. They immediately signed him to a £167 million deal. This made him the highest-paid teenage player ever. As a member of PSG, Mbappé continued his path to greatness.

"It was hard for me to be famous very young," he said. As always, his parents were a great help. "They were there for me and they say stay calm, stay with your values."

FACT

In addition to his native language of French, Mbappé speaks English and Spanish fluently. He speaks some Portuguese and Italian as well.

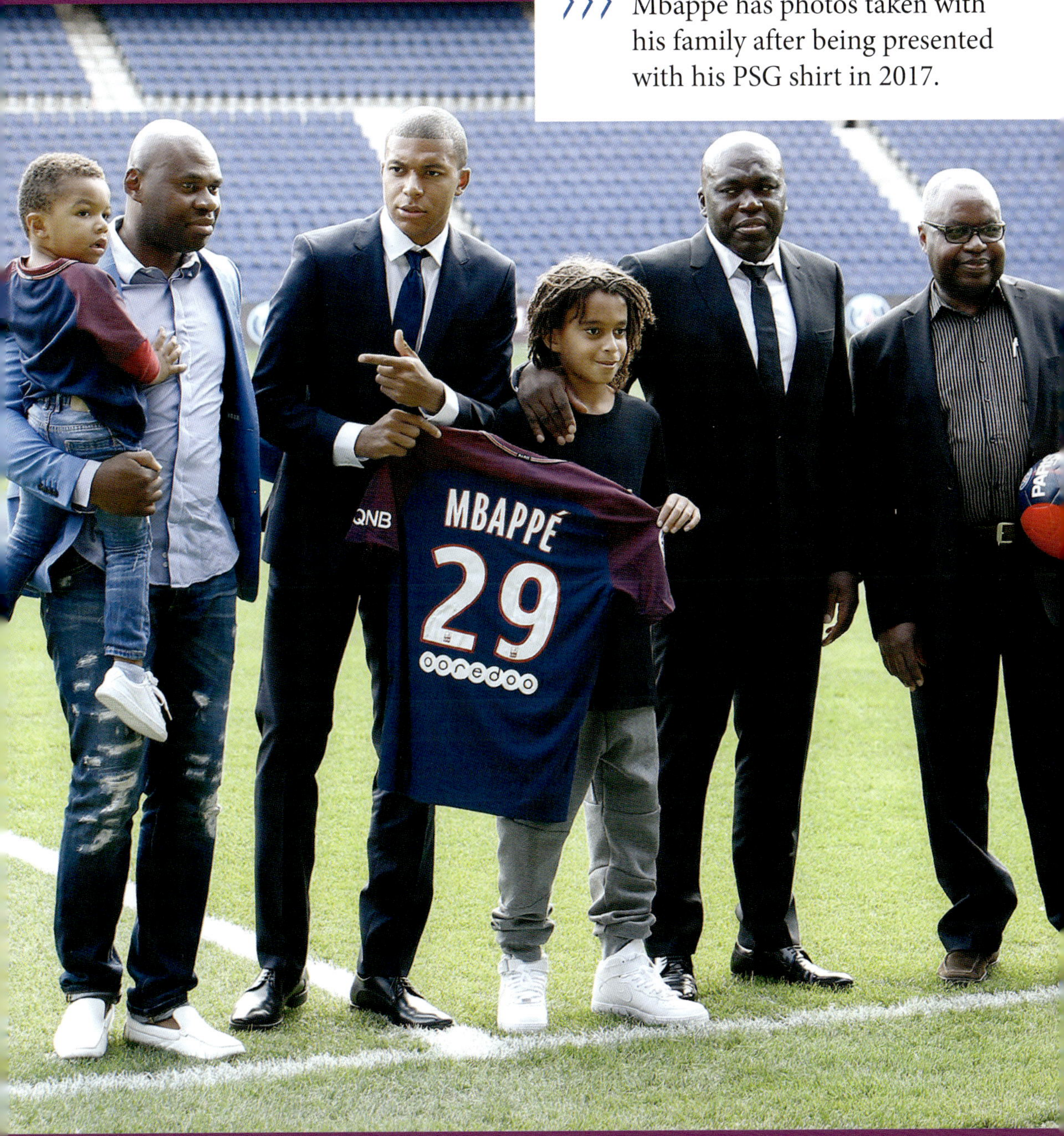

››› Mbappé has photos taken with his family after being presented with his PSG shirt in 2017.

CHAPTER THREE

SUPERSTAR SUCCESS

Mbappé's success with PSG soon translated to the international stage. In 2018, he was chosen to represent France in the FIFA World Cup in Russia. This selection was a huge honour.

Despite being only 19, Mbappé scored four goals, including the one in the final against Croatia. Not only did he help France win their second-ever World Cup, but he also won the FIFA World Cup Best Young Player award.

From his earliest years, Mbappé wanted to do more and push limits. So it was no surprise when he said, "It was not the end when I won the World Cup. It was the first chapter of something crazy."

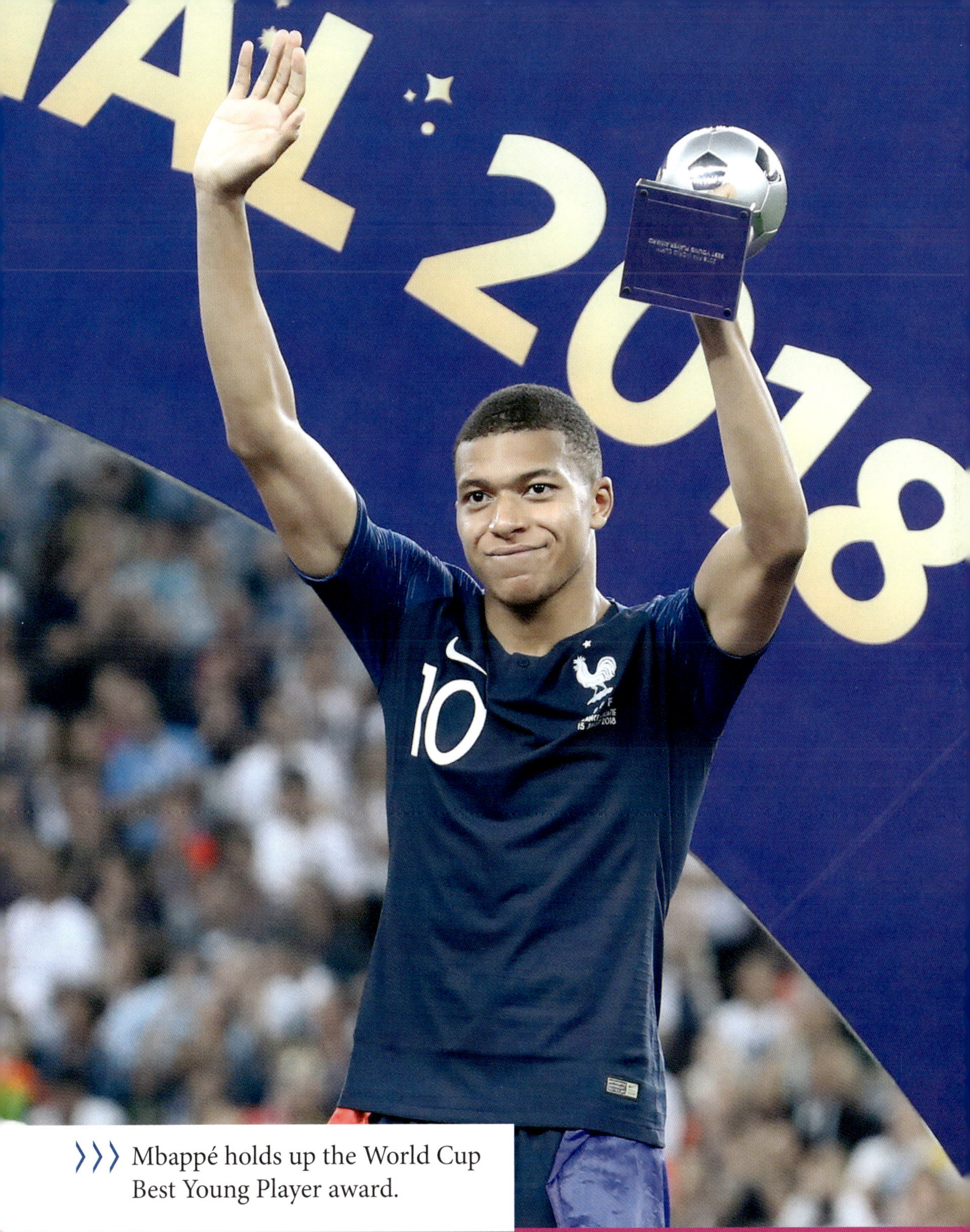

››› Mbappé holds up the World Cup Best Young Player award.

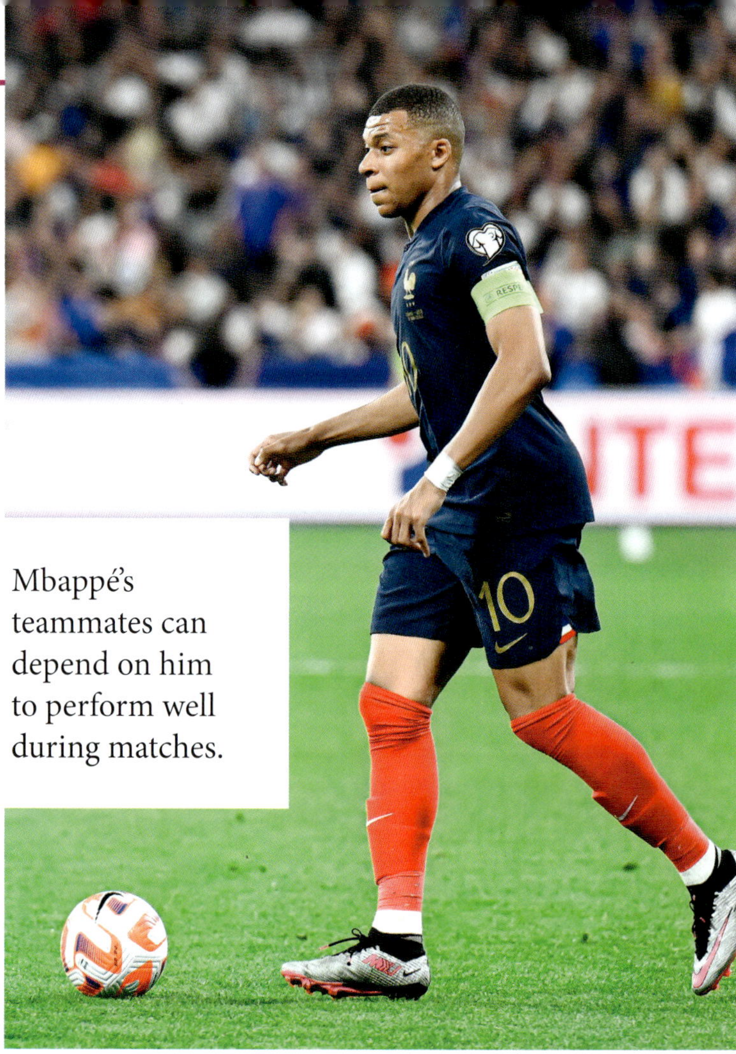

〉〉〉 Mbappé's teammates can depend on him to perform well during matches.

Over the next few years, Mbappé's success was amazing. He became the top goalscorer 10 times, with his highest goal count reaching 29. He also became the French Footballer of the Year three times. His amazing performance helped PSG become French champions six times and win the French Cup three times. He won the Player of the Year award four seasons in row.

This success paid off. Mbappé earned a new three-year deal worth more than £200 million. It made him the highest-paid footballer in the world.

When it was time for the 2022 World Cup, everyone had the same question: would Mbappé lead France to back-to-back World Cup victories?

FACT

Mbappé has a well-known trainer obsession. It began with a pair of Nike Air Max 1 trainers.

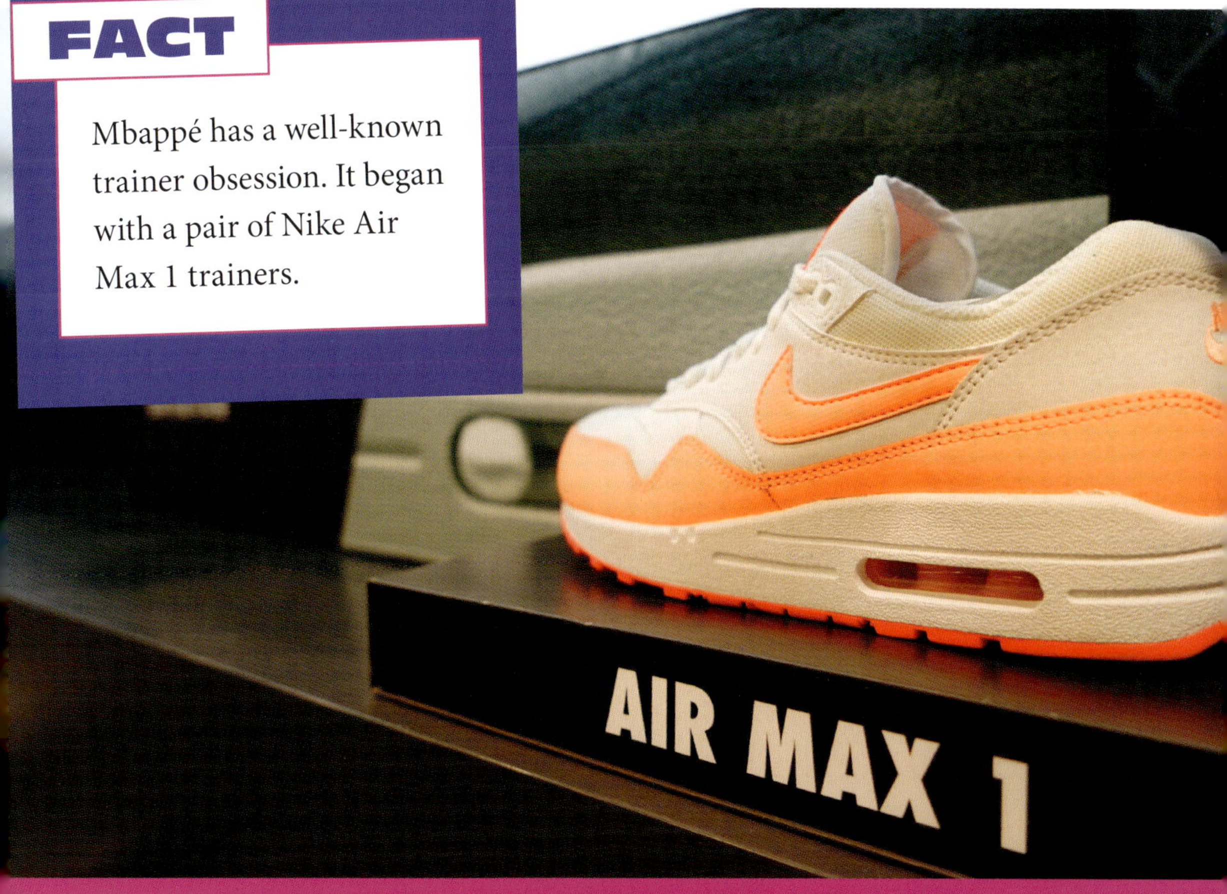

Mbappé started strong in the 2022 World Cup. He fired off five goals in the matches leading up to the final. But France's opponent, Argentina, had its own superstar. This superstar was Lionel Messi.

In what many call the greatest World Cup match ever, the lead went back and forth. Mbappé scored three goals, but the score was 3–3 at full time. After extra time, there was a **penalty shoot-out**. Argentina ended up winning the match 4–2 on penalties.

Soon after that disappointing loss, Mbappé shifted his focus to the 2026 World Cup. "We will return," he tweeted.

So many options

Mbappé could have played for three different countries in the World Cup. His mother is Algerian. His father is from Cameroon. He was born in France. His loyalty remained with the place he was born and raised – France.

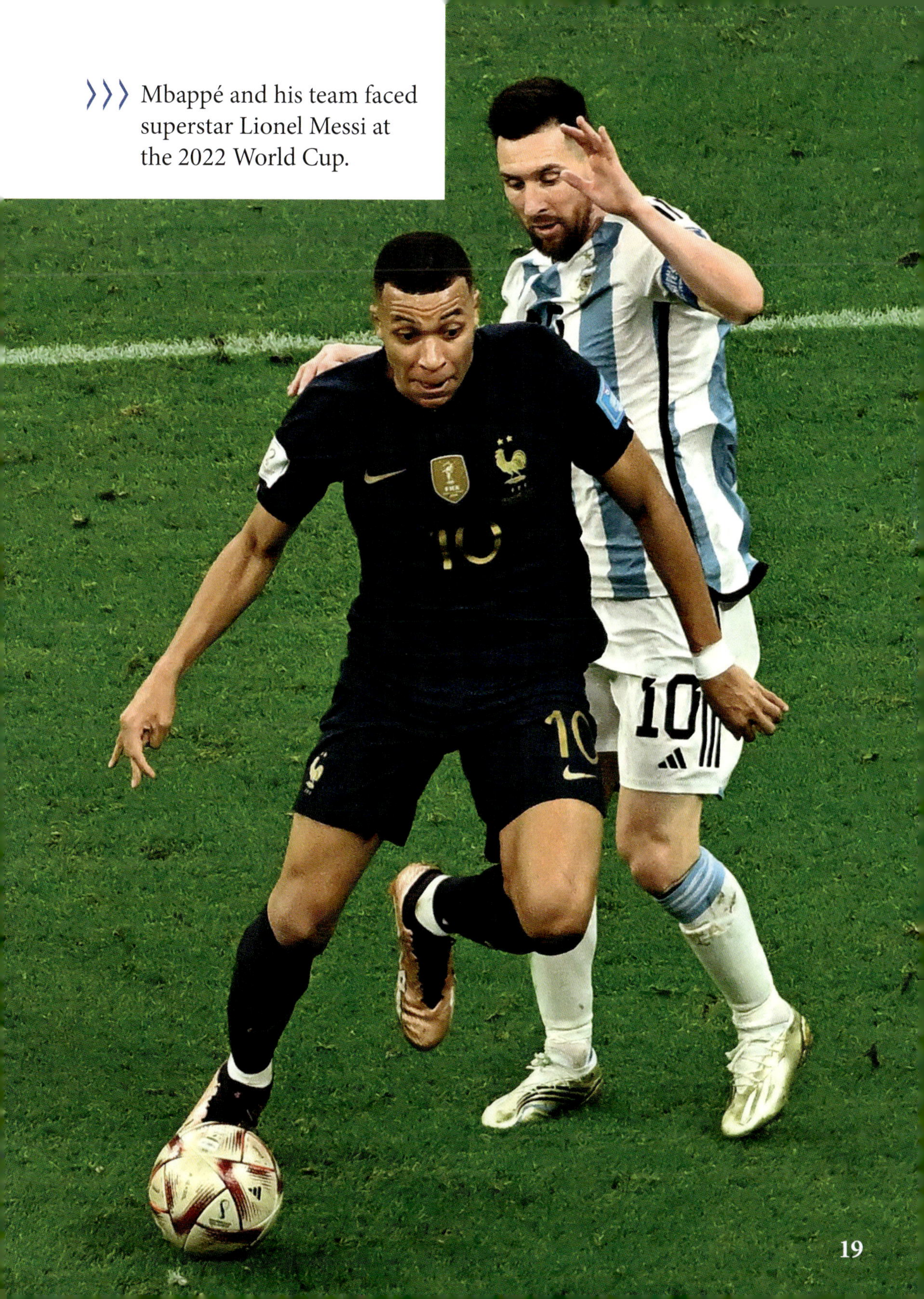

Mbappé and his team faced superstar Lionel Messi at the 2022 World Cup.

CHAPTER FOUR

A WINNER ON AND OFF THE PITCH

Mbappé is admired for his skills on the pitch, which include more than his physical movements. He is admired for his exceptional sportsmanship. He always supports his teammates. He celebrates all of their victories. He encourages them during challenging times.

But it's not just his own team that he respects. Mbappé has **consoled** opponents after tough matches too. He shows that true sportsmanship is more than winning or losing.

Mbappé understands that the power of sport can change lives. He uses his platform to make a positive impact wherever he can. He works with organizations like Premiers de Cordée. This organization coordinates sporting activities for children with disabilities.

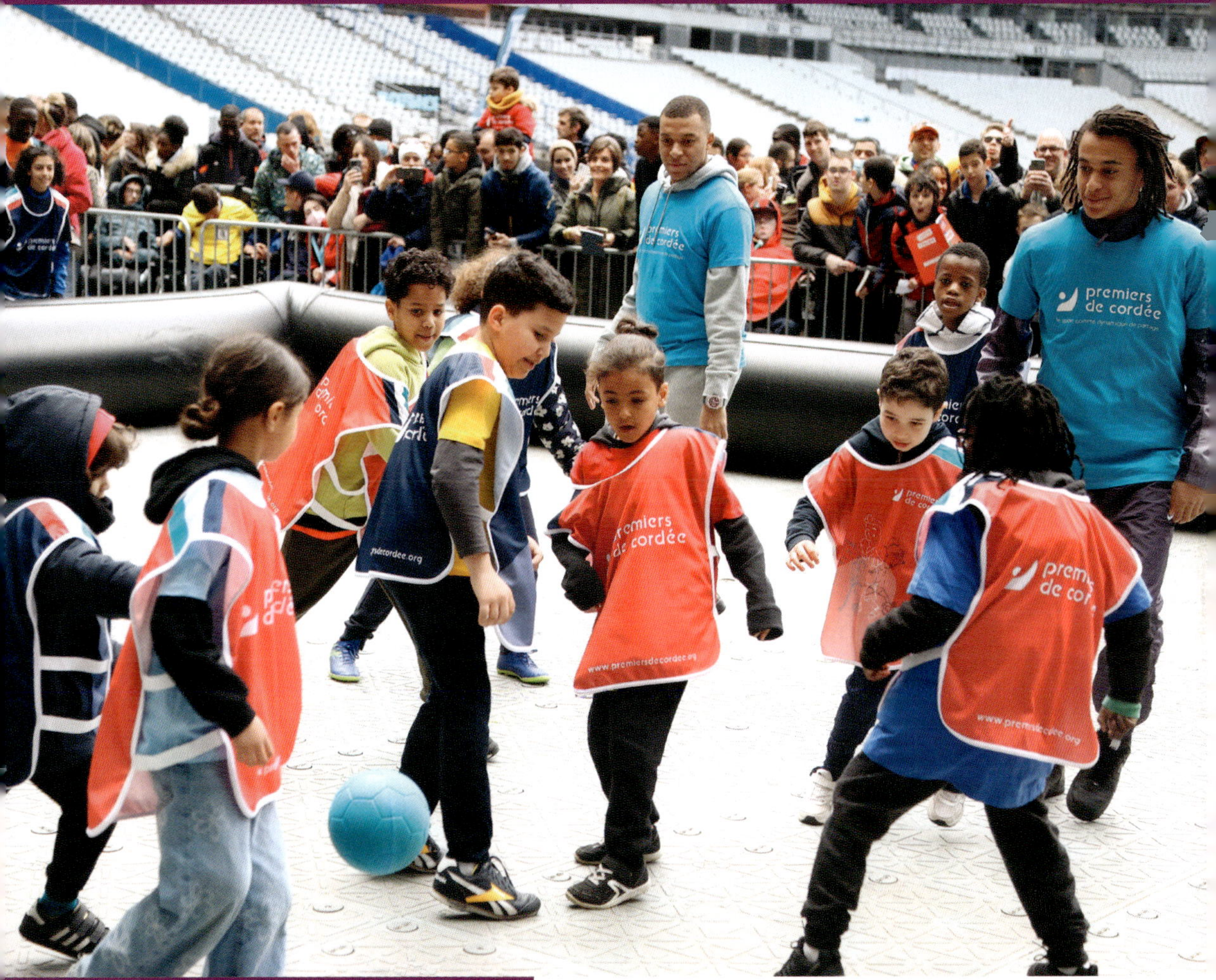

Mbappé and his brother Ethan work with children at a Premiers de Cordée event.

Mbappé donated his 2018 World Cup earnings to a charity for children with disabilities. The amount was around £380,000. "It doesn't change my life, but it changes theirs," he said. "And if it can change theirs, it is a great pleasure."

In 2020, Mbappé launched Inspired by Kylian Mbappé (IBKM). This organization helps children achieve their dreams. How? By supporting them in whatever career path they choose.

His big heart extends to animals as well. In 2021, Mbappé and Chinese Olympic diving gold medallist Zhang Jiaqi became the godparents of twin pandas. The pandas were born at a zoo in France. The athletes hope to create awareness about endangered species.

FACT

In 2022, Mbappé launched Zebra Valley. This Los Angeles-based entertainment company creates cross-platform content to encourage global diversity.

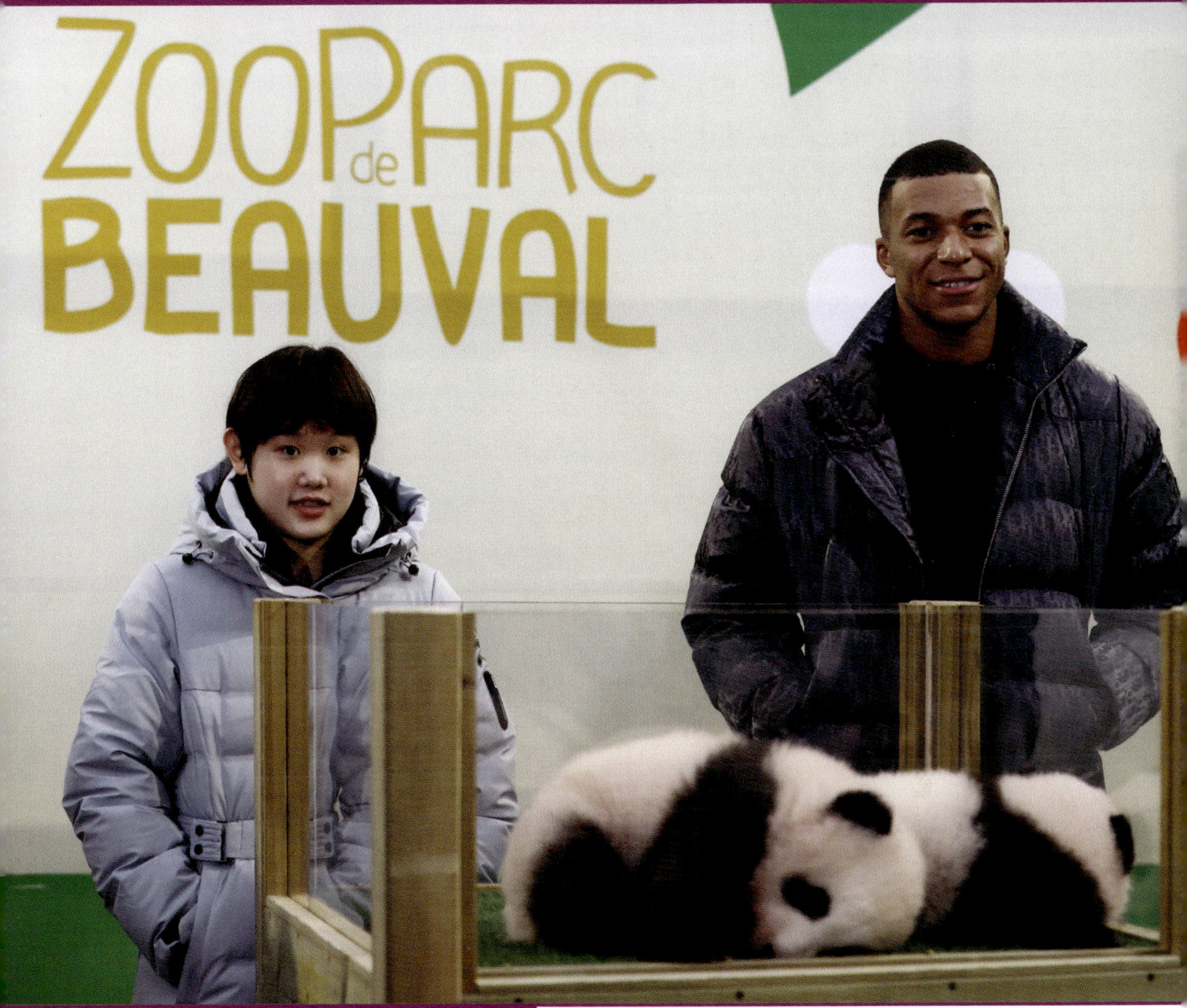

〉〉〉 Zhang Jiaqi and Mbappé pose with the twin panda cubs in 2021.

CHAPTER FIVE

THE BRIGHT FUTURE AHEAD

Mbappé's story is one of determination, talent and hard work. It's a reminder that success is not only measured by trophies and praise. It's also measured by the positive impact one can have on others.

Mbappé has already scored big in the world of football, and he's just getting started. Before turning 20, he was a global **icon**. He graced the cover of the video game *FIFA 2021*. That was a dream come true for a guy who loves the game.

As a child, Mbappé loved Real Madrid. In 2024, the dream to play for them became reality. He signed a five-year £12.8 million deal with the club. So what's next for the football icon? Maybe another World Cup or two.

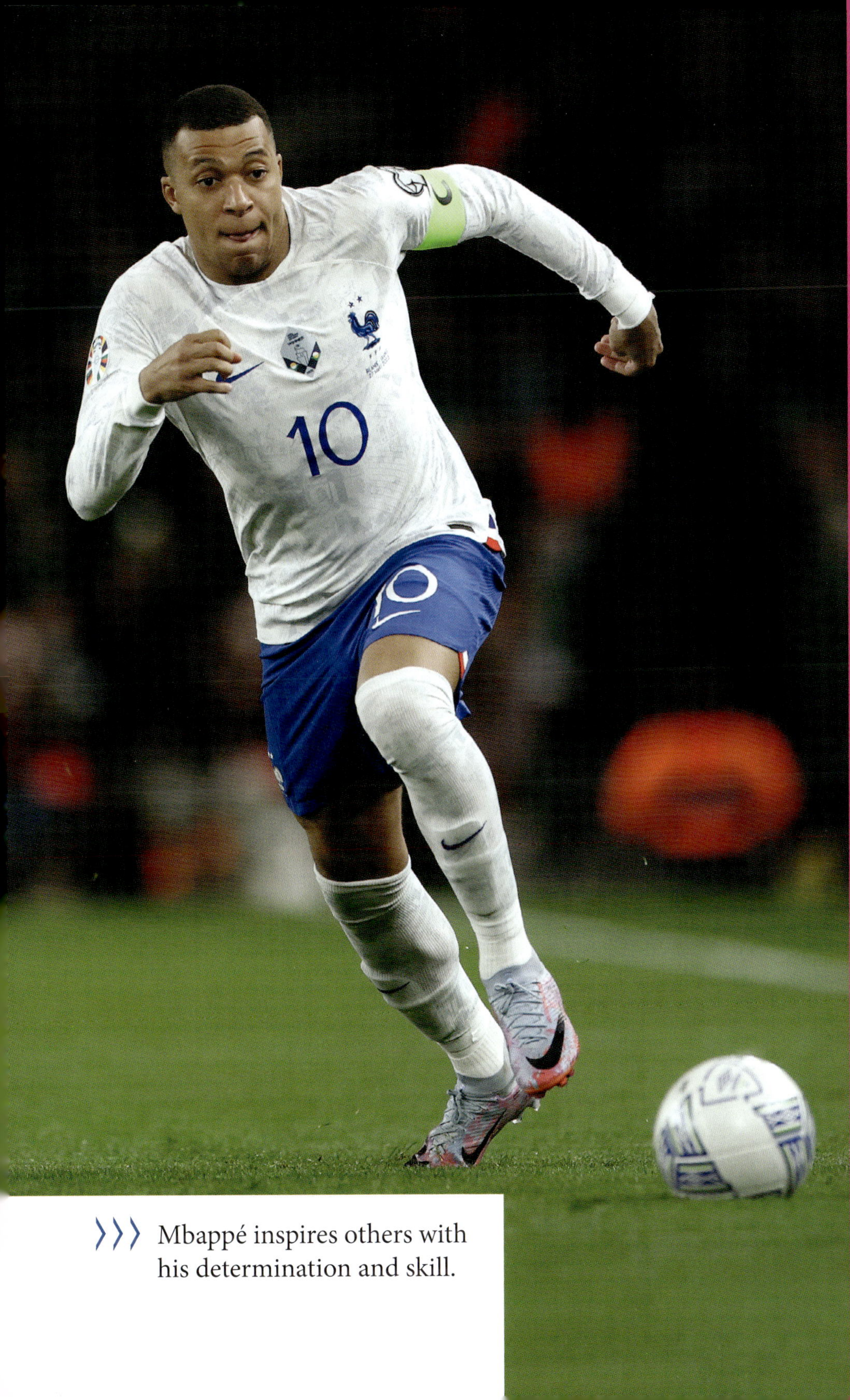

Mbappé inspires others with his determination and skill.

Mbappé also dreams of winning the Ballon d'Or award for the world's best footballer. It's one of the few awards he hasn't won yet.

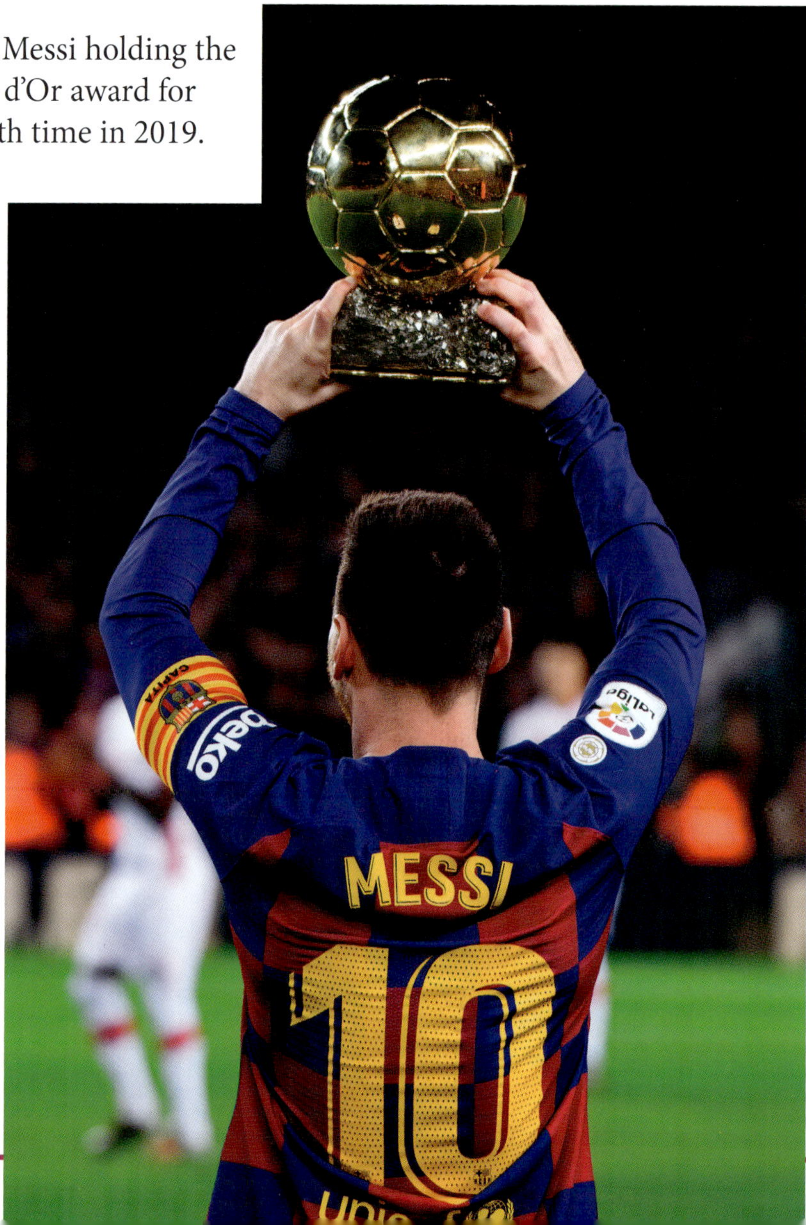

Lionel Messi holding the Ballon d'Or award for the sixth time in 2019.

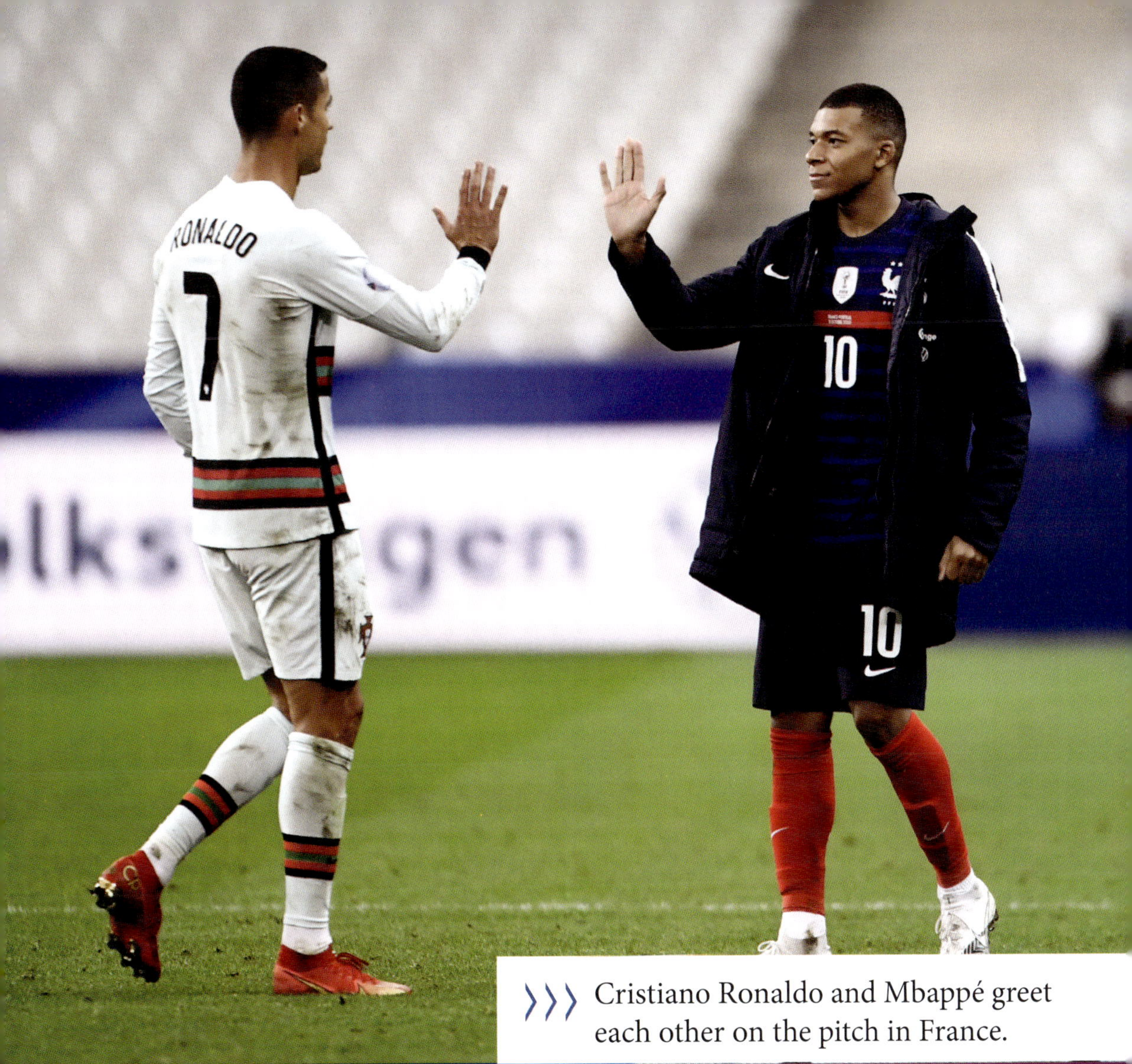

〉〉〉 Cristiano Ronaldo and Mbappé greet each other on the pitch in France.

Perhaps the most meaningful praise came from his childhood hero, football legend Cristiano Ronaldo: "Mbappé is the future and the present."

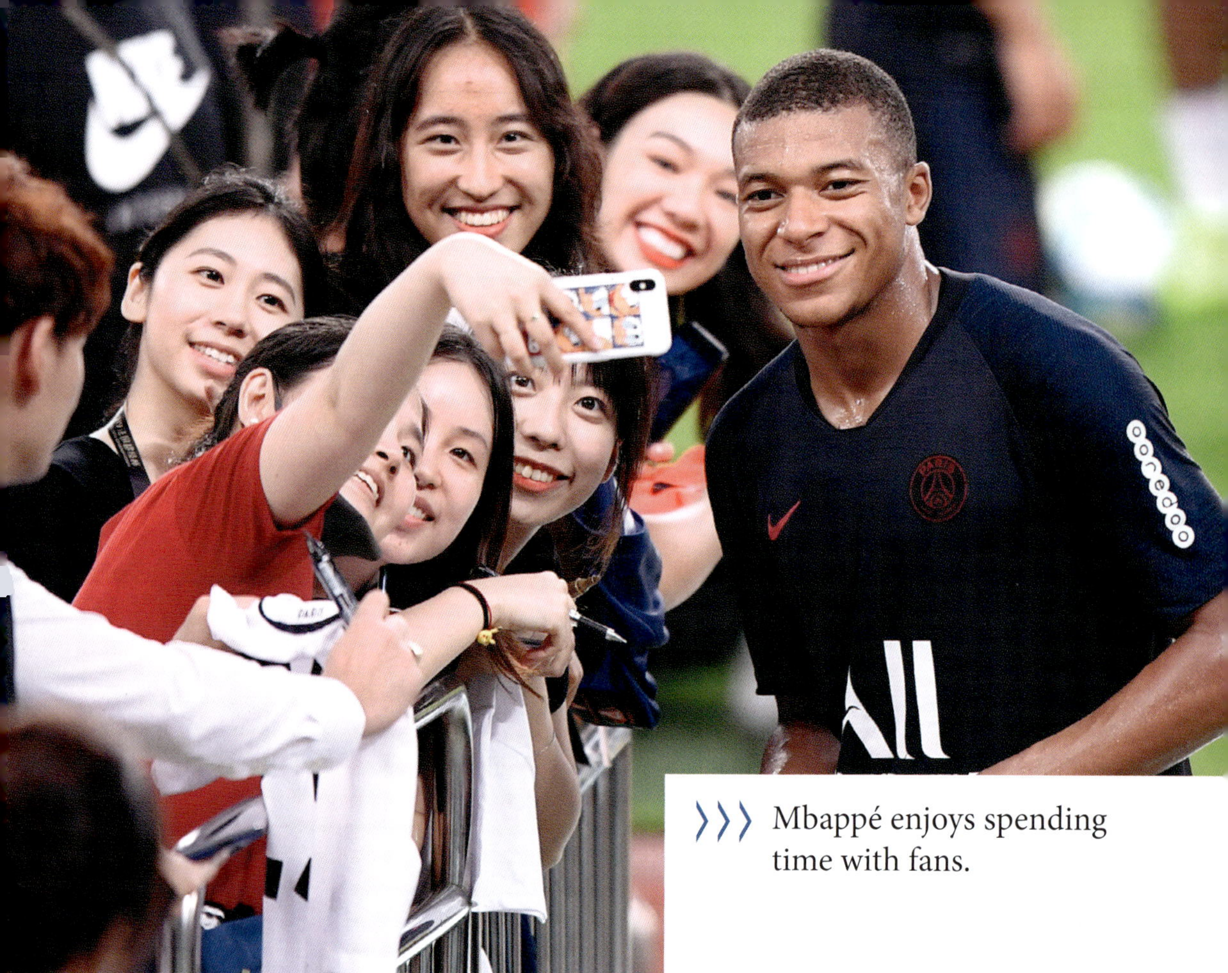

››› Mbappé enjoys spending time with fans.

Through it all, Mbappé stays humble. "I am aware of the risk with all the media attention, all the glitz and glamour around football," Mbappé said. "I know where I come from."

No matter where he goes or what he does, one thing is clear. As long as Mbappé stays true to himself and never loses sight of his roots, the future will remain as bright as his contagious smile.

TIMELINE

1998	Born in Paris, France, on 20 December
2004	Joins AS Bondy youth football team and is coached by his father
2011	Attends the prestigious Clairefontaine academy to train among top French football talent
2013	Joins AS Monaco youth academy, officially becoming a professional footballer
2015	Makes professional football debut for AS Monaco
2017	Wins Ligue 1 title with AS Monaco
2017	Transfers to Paris Saint-Germain (PSG)
2018	Wins FIFA World Cup with the French team; becomes youngest player to score in a World Cup final since Pelé
2018	Awarded the Legion of Honour with his team, France's highest order of merit
2020	Launches Inspired by Kylian Mbappé (IBKM)
2021	Wins UEFA Nations League; France becomes first nation to win this award, a World Cup and a European Championship
2021	Featured on cover of the video game *FIFA 2021*
2023	Named one of *Time* magazine's 100 Most Influential People in the World
2024	Signs contract with Real Madrid

GLOSSARY

AGENT person authorised to act on another's behalf

CONSOLE comfort

DEBUT first appearance or performance

DEFLECT bounce off

DRIBBLE move the ball along the ground with the feet

ICON person admired for having great influence on something

OPPONENT person who competes against another person

PENALTY SHOOT-OUT method used to determine the winner of a game tied after full time and extra time; players from each team take turns trying to score goals from the penalty spot

FIND OUT MORE

BOOKS

Football Legends 2024, David Ballheimer (Welbeck, 2023)

Kylian Mbappé (Football Rising Stars), Harry Meredith (Sweet Cherry Publishing, 2021)

Kylian Mbappé: The Ultimate Fan Book, Iain Spragg (Welbeck, 2020)

WEBSITES

www.bbc.co.uk/bitesize/articles/zkg2ywx
Try this true or false Mbappé quiz on the CBBC website.

www.bbc.co.uk/newsround/articles/c0dm1m8dlzeo
Read these Mbappé and Ronaldo facts.

www.realmadrid.com/en-US/football/first-team/players/kylian-mbappe
Find out about Mbappé's stats at Real Madrid.

INDEX

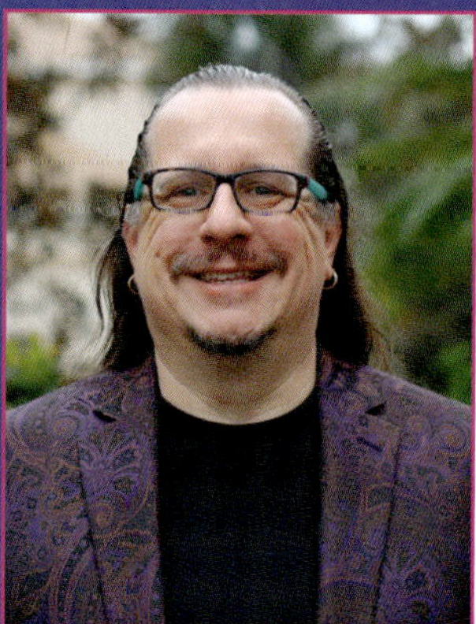

ABOUT THE AUTHOR

Ryan G. Van Cleave is the author of dozens of books for children and hundreds of articles published in magazines. As The Picture Book Whisperer, they help celebrities write books for children. Ryan lives in Florida, USA.